From Crisis to Confidence

Macroeconomics after the Crash

From Crisis to Confidence

Macroeconomics after the Crash

ROGER KOPPL

The Institute of Economic Affairs

First published in Great Britain in 2014 by
The Institute of Economic Affairs
2 Lord North Street
Westminster
London SW1P 3LB
in association with London Publishing Partnership Ltd
www.londonpublishingpartnership.co.uk

The mission of the Institute of Economic Affairs is to improve public understanding of the fundamental institutions of a free society, with particular reference to the role of markets in solving economic and social problems.

A CIP catalogue record for this book is available from the British Library.

ISBN 978-0-255-36693-9

Many IEA publications are translated into languages other than English or are reprinted. Permission to translate or to reprint should be sought from the Director General at the address above.

Typeset in Kepler by T&T Productions Ltd
www.tandtproductions.com

CONTENTS

THE AUTHOR

Roger Koppl is Professor of Finance in the Whitman School of Management at Syracuse University and a faculty fellow in the university's Forensic and National Security Sciences Institute. Koppl has served on the faculty of the Copenhagen Business School, Auburn University, Fairleigh Dickinson University and Auburn University at Montgomery. He has held visiting positions at George Mason University, New York University and Germany's Max Planck Institute of Economics. Professor Koppl is a past president of the Society for the Development of Austrian Economics. He is the editor of *Advances in Austrian Economics*.

Koppl's research addresses a variety of topics related to the unifying theme of economic epistemics. He is the author of *Big Players and the Economic Theory of Expectations* (Palgrave Macmillan, 2002). His research has appeared in the *Journal of Economic Perspectives*; the *Journal of Economic Behavior and Organization*; *Industrial and Corporate Change*; *Law, Probability and Risk*; *Criminology & Public Policy*; *Society*, and other scholarly journals. Koppl's research on forensic science has been featured in *Forbes* magazine, *Reason* magazine, *Slate*, *The Huffington Post* and other media outlets.

FOREWORD

Throughout its 60-year history, the IEA has made many contributions to the debate on what has come to be known as macroeconomics. The first Editorial Director, Arthur Seldon, brought to UK audiences the very different perspectives of authors such as Milton Friedman and Friedrich Hayek.

Some of Friedman's insights, expressed in IEA publications, had a profound practical effect on economic policy around the world. In particular, central banks stopped treating inflation and unemployment as variables that could be traded off against each other – a little more inflation being tolerated for a little less unemployment, for example. This belief that there was no long-run trade-off between inflation and unemployment was an important part of the rationale for establishing independent central banks. After all, if there is no benefit from high inflation, why not give responsibility for monetary policy to an independent agency so that politicians will not be tempted to create inflation for short-term gain? That way, the pursuit of low inflation would have more credibility as a policy and the markets would expect both lower and more stable inflation.

Of course, it has always been recognised that the economy does not adjust to shocks overnight and without any frictions. Wages may take time to adjust to lower levels of inflation, investment plans might be affected by the way in which increases in the money supply are transmitted through the system, and so on. This recognition – combined with the generally accepted belief that there was no long-run trade-off between inflation and output – led to the so-called neo-classical/new Keynesian consensus. This, in turn, accelerated the mathematisation of economics courses with university courses often focusing almost exclusively on a narrow category of models which attempted to describe credibility, leads and lags in the system, and so on.

Many students of economics – as well as many journalists and some politicians – see this treatment of economics as unhelpfully narrow, and discussion about the narrowness of many economics courses blossomed after the financial crash of 2008. A student group was set up at the University of Manchester called the Post-Crash Economics Society to make this very point and to request that economics courses be broadened.

Of course, the IEA has always had a wider perspective. It brought the works of F. A. Hayek and other Austrian economists to British academia and public policy circles many years ago. This excellent and timely monograph, *From Crisis to Confidence: Macroeconomics after the Crash*, is in that Austrian tradition. However, Roger Koppl's work is not so much an extension of Hayek's monetary theories as an attempt to help us understand the role that 'confidence' or – as Keynes put it – 'animal spirits' play in the economy and in the creation of boom and slump conditions.

Keynes talked about animal spirits but did not really provide a theory to explain how they operate. Why should animal spirits be high or low at any particular time? Why would some contrarian investors not take advantage of the fact that other investors have depressed animal spirits? Why will the depressed animal spirits of some investors not 'cancel out' the elevated animal spirits of others? Roger Koppl explains this by tying animal spirits in with the theory of 'Big Players' whose decisions can overwhelm the decisions of millions of entrepreneurs acting independently. Big Players tend to be organisations such as central banks and regulators whose actions can affect all market participants in a similar way. Koppl also draws on the recent empirical work on policy uncertainty that has been developing in recent years. Big Players may act in a way that suppresses animal spirits or leads them to get out of hand. The only way to deal with this problem is to curtail the influence of Big Players.

This monograph is an important contribution to the debate about the future of the discipline of economics. It seeks to broaden the discipline and thereby to increase its power to explain events such as the financial crash and the long slump that followed. Koppl's work takes us beyond the narrow perspectives that are often the focus of so many university courses and which form the basis of economic analysis in government and central banks. This Hobart Paper is also an important contribution to the current policy debate as we seek to explain the worst period for productivity in the modern economic history of the UK.

PHILIP BOOTH
Editorial and Programme Director
Institute of Economic Affairs
Professor of Insurance and Risk Management
Cass Business School, City University
May 2014

The views expressed in this monograph are, as in all IEA publications, those of the author and not those of the Institute (which has no corporate view), its managing trustees, Academic Advisory Council members or senior staff. With some exceptions, such as with the publication of lectures, all IEA monographs are blind peer reviewed by at least two academics or researchers who are experts in the field.

ACKNOWLEDGEMENTS

For comments and helpful discussion I thank Nicholas A. Bloom, Anthony Evans, Roger Garrison, Steve Horwitz and David Prychitko. I thank two anonymous referees, who provided unusually helpful and penetrating commentary on a preliminary draft. Earlier conversations with Bruno Prior and William J. Luther made an indirect contribution to this monograph, for which I thank them.

To Maria, who brings joy.

SUMMARY

- Since US output peaked in December 2007 growth has been anaemic and output remains below potential. In addition, US unemployment has been persistently high. It increased from 4.4 per cent in May of 2007 to 10 per cent in October 2009 and was still at 6.7 per cent at the beginning of 2014. The post-crash period is quite unlike typical post-war recession periods after which employment has generally recovered within about two years. This pattern has been followed in many EU countries too.
- The background to the long slump was a boom followed by a bust. Although the Federal Reserve seems to have pursued conventional monetary policy rules until 2002, from that point interest rates were kept too low for too long. This was an important policy mistake during the boom period.
- As well as mistakes in monetary policy, several complementary government failures ensured that the boom manifested itself disproportionately in the housing sector and encouraged excess risk taking in financial markets. The central underlying fact in the boom period, however, was loose monetary policy.
- Standard neo-classical macroeconomics does not have an adequate explanation for the slow pace of recovery

from the financial crash. Many other economists continue to argue that the problem is a deficiency of 'aggregate demand'. These economists want us to 'stimulate' our way out of the slump. However, repeated stimulatory measures have not effected a complete recovery. In the UK, for example, government borrowing has led the national debt to double in five years while output is still below potential.

- Arguably, the financial crisis itself should have been sufficient to call into question the standard neo-classical and new-Keynesian economic paradigms. HM Queen Elizabeth II asked economists at the LSE why nobody saw the crisis coming. This was a good question and the answer she received was inadequate.

- One aspect of economic theory which has been neglected is the concept of 'animal spirits' or 'confidence'. Keynes, and others before him, discussed the importance of these ideas without ever developing a proper theory or explaining why and how confidence or animal spirits might affect the economy.

- The state of confidence determines whether banks are willing to lend because the costs and risks that banks perceive are made up of both objective and subjective elements. If a weak state of confidence leads banks to over-estimate the costs and risks of lending, then banks will lend less than they otherwise would. Other economic actors are also affected by the state of confidence.

- Confidence is undermined by policy uncertainty and the ability for 'Big Players' to unduly influence the economic system. Big Players include governments, monetary authorities and regulators, though there can also be Big Players in the private sector. Policy uncertainty increased after the financial crash and the evidence suggests that this affected investment and growth. For example, Baker et al. (2013) show that the increase in policy uncertainty in the US from 2006 to 2011 probably caused a persistent fall in real industrial production reaching as high as 2.5 per cent at one point. Also, after the crash, the UK suffered a productivity shock unprecedented in its industrial history. This was coincident with the top 100 British businesses increasing their cash holdings by over £42bn (34 per cent) in the five years to the autumn of 2013.

- Recent regulatory developments such as the Dodd–Frank Act violate the principle of the rule of law and therefore undermine confidence and increase policy uncertainty. For example, the Dodd–Frank Act will almost certainly be subject to arbitrariness in its implementation and firms will not be able to plan in advance knowing the legal consequences of their actions.

- In order to restore and maintain confidence, we need an economic constitution. This constitution needs three elements. Firstly, there must be long-term fiscal discipline: investors must know that they can plan for the long term without either taxation or borrowing getting out of hand. Secondly, the role of Big Players must be reduced. Finally, we need monetary competition and regulatory competition. Regulation should not be the responsibility of state bodies with considerable discretionary power.

FIGURES

1   INTRODUCTION

The state of confidence, as they term it, is a matter to which practical men always pay the closest and most anxious attention. But economists have not analysed it carefully and have been content, as a rule, to discuss it in general terms.

J. M. Keynes

To investigate in what conditions what type of expectations is likely to have a stabilising or destabilising influence is no doubt one of the next tasks of dynamic theory. We submit that it cannot be successfully tackled unless expectations are made the subject of causal explanation.

Ludwig M. Lachmann

Economic thought and policy are both moving towards command and control. There is a reason for this dangerous trend. The Great Recession, as the current crisis has been called, looks to many observers like a failure of markets brought on by insufficient regulation. In a common view, financial market deregulation brought on an irrational frenzy of excess capitalism and unrestrained greed. It was 'bankers gone wild' as Paul Krugman (2012) has put it. If bankers go wild, we need sober regulators to control them. But if I am right to think the interventionist turn is mistaken, then we need to know why. We need to know what has gone wrong with the economy and what has gone wrong with economics. If intervention and 'stimulus' are not the answer, what is?

It is worth noting the background at the time of writing because in some countries there is a degree of optimism that the crisis is over. However, though growth has resumed in the US and the UK, other countries still stagnate – especially in the euro zone. And, even in those countries that are growing again, there are concerns about long-term secular stagnation. Furthermore, none of the major crisis countries are close to trend national income levels again: recovery has been anaemic.

The stakes are high because, if we respond to the crisis and anaemic growth by 'more regulation', things can go wrong. We took an interventionist turn in the Great Depression too, which goes a long way to explaining why it dragged out so long (Higgs 1997). Freer trade after the war contributed to relative economic stability at the time in spite of interventionist measures largely inherited from the Great Depression. Economic thinking eventually began to turn away from interventionism, partly because of the work of economists such as F. A. Hayek and Milton Friedman. Changes in economic policy followed this change in economic *thinking*. These changes were so profound that Andrei Shleifer (2009) could describe the period from 1980 to 2005 as 'The Age of Milton Friedman'.

The global move toward sound money, free trade and individual choice coincided with a marked improvement in human welfare. Between 1980 and 2005, the world's real per capita income grew over 57 per cent, roughly 2 per cent per year (Shleifer 2009: 124). Infant mortality fell almost 42 per cent over the same period (p. 124). Average schooling grew from 4.4 years in 1980 to almost six years in 1999 (p. 124). 'Between 1980 and 2000, the share of the world's population living on less than $1 a day fell from 34.8 per cent to 19 per cent' (p. 125). As Israel Kirzner taught, 'Economics is a matter of life and death.' Economic liberalism, free trade and sound money saved lives in the age of Milton Friedman, and the world became a better place.

Today's interventionist tendencies threaten this global improvement in human well-being. But so do the economic problems that prompted them. If the Great Recession is a market failure, we may need to reconsider the sort of economic thinking that gave us the age of Milton Friedman. But if the Great Recession was more government failure than market failure, then we need to resist and reverse the turn towards intervention. A few facts may help to suggest why the Great Recession matters so much for our preferences in economic policy.

The nature of the Great Recession in brief

Output in the US peaked in December 2007. By a commonly used criterion, the recession ended when national income finally bottomed out in June 2009 around 5 per cent below its peak. But output has remained sluggish since then and, more importantly, unemployment has been persistently high. Unemployment in the US moved from 4.4

Figure 1 **Percentage job losses in US post-war recessions**

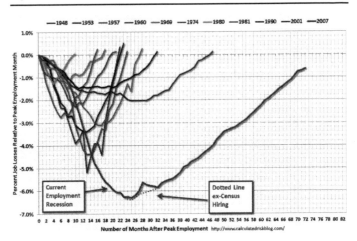

Reproduced by kind permission of Calculatedriskblog.com

per cent in May 2007 to 10 per cent in October 2009. In June 2013 the measured unemployment rate was still high at 7.8 per cent. Youth unemployment in June 2013 was 27 per cent in the US and 21 per cent in the UK. In April 2013 Spain recorded an unemployment rate of 27 per cent and a youth unemployment rate of 57 per cent. These dreadful numbers understate the problem because many potential workers have left the labour market. In the US, the ratio of employment to population fell 4 percentage points from 63 per cent in December 2007 to 59 per cent in June 2013. The same ratio in the UK slipped from about 60 per cent to about 58 per cent. In Italy, the ratio of employment to population fell from 46 per cent in 2006 and 2007 to less than 44 per cent by the end of 2011.

Figure 2 **US real gross domestic product and real potential gross domestic product**

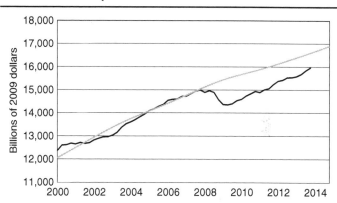

Recovery has been slow, as Figure 1 illustrates. For each of the post-war recessions in the US, the graph plots the percentage job loss from that cycle's peak employment against the number of months that have passed since that peak. In a typical post-war recession, employment recovers within about two years. The last two recessions are the two exceptions. In March 2013, after over five years of the Great Recession, employment levels were *still* below their peak of January 2008 (output peaked about a month before employment peaked). As Figure 2 illustrates, output in the US finally crawled back to its pre-recession peak after about four years, but remains well below its long-run trend as measured by 'potential GDP'. In the UK, the level of GDP had yet to return to its pre-recession peak by June 2013, as Figure 3 illustrates, never mind its long-run trend.

Figure 3 **Real UK GDP (£m 2010) vs UK GDP long-term trend extrapolated**

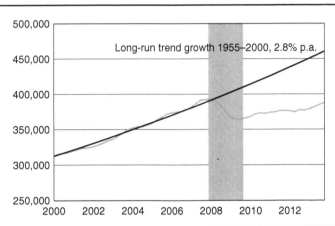

What went wrong?

Things have gone badly wrong. The current large, long-lasting limits to economic prosperity suggest the need for change. We need a new direction in economic theory and policy alike. But which direction is the best way forward?

If we are to strike out in the right direction, we need to know what happened. If we diagnose the problem correctly, we might be able to prescribe the right medicine. If we give a false diagnosis, we will probably prescribe the wrong medicine and make the patient even sicker. At one level there is fairly broad agreement about what happened: we had a credit crisis. Somehow there came to be a lot of bad debt in the system that at first looked good. When housing prices fell, so too did the scales from our eyes. All that debt that had been looking good suddenly looked very bad. The resulting cascade of credit defaults and bankruptcies brought with it unemployment and reduced output. The boom ended in a bust. On this economists agree. But economists are not agreed on how the credit bubble came about in the first place or why the slump has dragged on.

There are two main theories of why we had a credit bubble, and we might as well call them 'Keynesian' and 'Austrian'. In the Keynesian story, there is an irrational expansion of credit, perhaps because creditors under-estimate the risks they are taking. Paul Krugman represents this view rather well. In good economic times 'debt looks safe' and 'the memory of the bad things debt can do fades into the mists of history. Over time, the perception that debt is safe leads to more relaxed lending standards' (Krugman 2012: 48). Eventually, bankers will become complacent and forgetful, at which point they start making a lot of bad loans. With all that bad debt, there must come a moment of crisis, which Paul McCulley has dubbed the 'Minsky moment' (Lahart 2007). Such a moment is 'the point at which excess leverage cannot be sustained and the system unravels' (McCulley 2009). It is called the 'Minsky moment' because the idea of such 'financial fragility' comes from the Keynesian economist Hyman Minsky, whom Krugman cites. Janet Yellen tells a similar tale when she calls the crisis a 'Minsky meltdown', although she admits that 'Fed monetary policy may also have contributed to the U.S. credit boom' (2009: 3).

Krugman (2012), Yellen (2009) and others have used the terms such as 'Minsky moment' and 'Minsky meltdown' to suggest that the crisis is an example of market failure. The basic idea is that we had deregulation of financial markets in the US and elsewhere, which led to a lot of irresponsible lending and, ultimately, a credit crisis. The 'combination of deregulation and failure to keep regulations updated', Krugman explains, 'was a big factor in the debt surge and the crisis the followed' (2012: 56). It is true that there was a kind of selective deregulation before the crisis. But the idea that excess lending was somehow a market failure overlooks a big important fact: too big to fail. The bankers were gambling with other people's money. As I discuss below, they had plenty of incentive to lower their lending standards. And if the bottom falls out? Well, we will get a bailout.

A recent scandal in Ireland suggests how nominally private banks may view bailouts as a tool of their trade. Ireland's Anglo Irish Bank was in immediate danger at the time of the 2008 financial crisis. In September 2008 two of the bank's executives, John Bowie and Peter Fitzgerald had a phone call to discuss what to do, and the call was recorded. Bowe explains to Fitzgerald that they had met with the Irish regulator the day before and asked for a €7 billion bailout that would be a bridge between the current moment of illiquidity and a future moment in which the bank will have shored up its position and will be able to start repaying the loan. Bowie explains that he had asked for '€7 billion bridging'. Fitzgerald then elaborates: 'So ... so it is bridged until we can pay you back ... which is never'. At this remark, both laugh.

Thus, the officers of the Anglo Irish Bank seem to have indicated to the regulator that they intended to repay a

Figure 4 **Excess reserves of depository institutions**

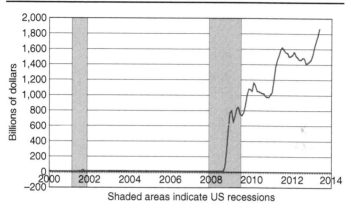

Shaded areas indicate US recessions

Data: Board of Governors of the Federal Reserve System

debt they knew they would not, in fact, repay. A bit later in the conversation, Bowie explains that they needed much more than €7 billion, but chose to ask for that much to lure the regulator into a series of piecemeal bailouts. He says: 'The strategy here is you pull them in, you get them to write a big [cheque] and they have to keep, they have to support their money, you know.' And, 'If they saw, if they saw, the enormity of it up front, they might decide, they might decide they have a choice. You know what I mean? They might say the cost to the taxpayer is too high. But ... em ... if it doesn't look too big at the outset ... if it looks big, big enough to be important, but not too big that it kind of spoils everything...' This conversation suggests that the 'moral hazard' problem created by 'too big to fail' is quite real and something that directly and self-consciously influences the thinking of financial institutions. It hardly seems reasonable to call such gaming of the regulators 'market failure'.

There is another problem with the 'bankers gone wild' hypothesis that does not take proper account of the context in which they were operating. From where did these wild bankers get the funds to lend? There was a credit boom and not just a decline in lending standards. Figure 4 shows the level of excess reserves in US banks from 2000 to 2012. Before the recession they were flat. Thus, banks were not keeping fewer reserves in order to make more loans: they were able to make more loans because they had more reserves.

I will offer a more or less 'Austrian' explanation of the boom in which a central bank policy of easy money injects credit into the system, but without any corresponding saving by households. Financial markets get a false signal that credit has become more abundant and cheap. As we shall see, an 'Austrian' story of this sort is told by some figures who are not usually considered Austrian. Borrowing from John Taylor (2009) and others, I will show that the central banks inappropriately and needlessly expanded the volume of credit in the years before the boom, thus ensuring a subsequent bust. It was not bankers gone wild that caused the unsustainable boom; it was *central* bankers gone wild.

There are also 'Austrian' and 'Keynesian' explanations for the long slump that followed the bust. In the Keynesian interpretation of Paul Krugman, 'this depression is gratuitous ... it is the result of nothing more fundamental than inadequate demand' (2012, location 67). Krugman himself emphasises the simplicity of his view that 'stimulus' is good and 'austerity' is bad: 'Big economic problems can sometimes have simple, easy solutions' (2012: 30). The bust caused a fall in aggregate demand, and we will languish in the slump until we get enough government 'stimulus' to restore aggregate demand.

Although I believe Krugman is wrong to think that we can spend our way out of the current slump, it may well be that greater monetary ease would have been helpful after the bust. In the bust there can occur what Hayek called a 'secondary depression' in which 'unemployment may itself become the cause of an absolute shrinkage of aggregate demand which in turn may bring about a further increase of unemployment and thus lead to a cumulative process of contraction in which unemployment feeds on unemployment.' This sort of self-reinforcing collapse 'should of course be prevented by appropriate monetary countermeasures' (Hayek 1978: 210). The moment of crisis is not the moment for monetary stringency.[1]

---

1 In 1978 Hayek said: 'Though I am sometimes accused of having represented the deflationary cause of the business cycles as part of the curative process, I do not think that was ever what I argued' (Hayek 1978: 210). And yet Krugman calls Hayek a member of the 'liquidationist school, which basically asserted that the suffering that takes place in a depression is good and natural and that nothing should be done to alleviate it' (Krugman 2012: 204–5). The reader may judge whether Hayek or Krugman characterised Hayek's position correctly.

After the bust: confidence, uncertain rules of the game and 'Big Players'

It is not obvious whether we had monetary stringency or ease after the bust. In the US, the Federal Reserve (the Fed) rapidly expanded the so-called monetary base, which is made up of the reserves banks have available to pay off any depositors who might want to withdraw funds plus paper money in the hands of the public. The financial crisis struck in September of 2008, and the monetary base in the US had doubled by the end of the year. This seems a monumental increase sure to bring inflation with it. But more than 90 per cent of that increase became an increase in banks' excess reserves. The banks took the money and sat on it. They did so in part because the Fed began paying the interest on reserves to banks in October 2008. In other words, at the moment of financial crisis and collapsing credit the American central bank began paying commercial banks to *not* lend money. The Federal Reserve's policy of 'quantitative easing' may have been too loose. But quantitative easing came together with the paying of interest on reserves. Thus, it may well be that Fed policy has been too tight. In either event, however, the system has had time to adjust to the new regime, and yet output and employment have been stuck in a five-year slump. Whether we should fault the Fed for monetary stringency or not, the system has shown a curious inability to adjust.

The Keynesian view that we just need more stimulus depends on the idea that markets are slow to adjust. Usually the claim is that *prices* are slow to adjust. Unemployment exists because wages are slow to fall after the bust. But wages have now had five years to adjust and we still have high unemployment. Sometimes the claim is that *quantities*, not prices, are slow to adjust. In this version of slow adjustment, flexible prices will not help because your spending is my income. Paraphrasing Robert Clower (1965): I would like to hire you to work in my vineyard, but I cannot pay your wages because nobody is buying my champagne. And you would like to buy my champagne, but you cannot pay for it because nobody at the vineyard has hired you to work in it. Something like this champagne problem (as we may call it) probably has slowed adjustment after the bust. But we have had over five years for entrepreneurs to realise that they might front workers their wages, harvest the grapes and sell champagne to those same workers for a profit. In other words, there has been plenty of time to make the required 'structural' adjustments. The much greater economic adjustments required after World War II were made quickly: rapid adjustment *is* possible. Today, however, adjustment is slow and output is low. Somehow, something is inhibiting adjustment. That something, I would argue, is the state of confidence.

My 'Austrian' explanation of the long slump will be that policy uncertainty has created a low state of confidence and a corresponding slump in investment. The 'state of confidence' has a long history in economics, as I will show. Economists today are more likely to speak of 'animal spirits' than 'confidence' to identify the same supposed dispositions, expectations and emotions of business investors. Whatever the label, it is an important topic. And yet there has been relatively little attention to the theory of the state of confidence. Drawing on Higgs (1997) and Koppl (2002), I will outline a theory of confidence that explains the long slump, a theory that fills in the something that has inhibited economic adjustment after the boom.

In brief, the explanation is as follows. Interventionist policies create uncertainty, raise the costs of financial intermediation and discourage investment. I might almost say that the problem is not that the government has done too little, but that it has done too much. That way of putting it, though, may seem to suggest that I am an 'austerian' who wants to heat up the economy by freezing government spending. The problem, however, is not the level of government spending. The problem is changing rules, uncertain regulations, shifting Fed policy. The problem is the variability and unpredictability of government economic policy.

In the theory I lay out below, the state of confidence is more likely to be arbitrary and self-referencing the more precarious our knowledge of the future. Investor expectations are never certain (by their nature) and never a total blank. Where we are between the poles of ignorance and prescience depends on the policy regime affecting investors. I will emphasise two aspects of the policy regime: whether the rules of the game are uncertain and whether there is 'Big Player' influence.

Rules of the game

The 'rules of the game' are the rules of economic exchange. They include tax law, the law of contract and regulations. If the rules of the game are ambiguous or changeable, investors experience uncertainty and ignorance of the future. If the rules of the game are known and stable, investors experience greater prescience. They have greater confidence in their guesses about the future. Irregular and arbitrary taxes, for example, make it harder to estimate the prospective profit of alternative investments; a simple regular and transparent tax code eliminates one source of uncertainty, helping investors to formulate a serviceable, if not perfectly strict, mathematical expectation of prospective yields. Robert Higgs (1997) has coined the term 'regime uncertainty' to describe situations in which the rules of the game are uncertain. As we shall see, regime uncertainty discourages investment (regime uncertainty is the cause, reduced investment the effect).

Big Players

Big Players are economic actors with three characteristics. Firstly, they are big enough to influence the market or markets in question. Secondly, they are largely immune from the discipline of profit and loss. Thirdly, they act on discretion and are not bound by any simple rules. Activist central bankers are paradigmatic Big Players. A private actor might be a Big Player, but only in the relatively short run or if it is a protected monopoly. As I argue below, Big Players are hard to predict. They reduce the reliability of economic expectations, which encourages both herding and contrarianism in financial markets. Big Player influence drives investors towards greater ignorance and uncertainty. For example, discretionary monetary policy makes it hard to estimate the future purchasing power of the currency and, therefore, the value of alternative investments: a simple monetary rule eliminates one source of uncertainty, helping investors to formulate a serviceable mathematical expectation of prospective yields. Koppl (2002) has developed the theory of Big Players and I will draw on that and related work in this monograph.

When there is Big Player influence or regime uncertainty investors become more ignorant, less prescient. As they grow more ignorant their investment decisions cannot depend as fully on strict mathematical expectation, since the basis for making such calculations is correspondingly weakened. They are more likely to follow the crowd and to base their decisions on an overall sense of optimism or pessimism rather than independent judgements of prospective yield. In these circumstances, the state of confidence becomes more arbitrary and more self-referential. More or less arbitrary swings of optimism and pessimism are now more likely. Regime uncertainty and Big Players make the economy look more Keynesian as it is more dependent on 'animal spirits' rather than economic calculation, which becomes more difficult. As we shall see, there is a sense in which Big Players and regime uncertainty reflect 'Keynesian' policies, which suggests the self-defeating nature of Keynesian macroeconomic policy: Keynesian policies tend to create a Keynesian economy.

When the recent financial crisis turned acute in the autumn of 2008 the US, the UK and other nations turned towards more interventionist policies. Two remarks by

President Bush characterise the interventionist turn in economic policy. In December 2008 he said, 'I've abandoned free-market principles to save the free-market system' (AFP 2008). And the following January, shortly before leaving office, he said: 'I readily concede I chucked aside my free-market principles when I was told ... the situation we were facing could be worse than the Great Depression' (UPI 2009). Unfortunately, the policies adopted after free-market principles were 'chucked aside' increased Big Player influence and regime uncertainty, thus throwing the world economy into a kind of Keynesian funk from which it has yet to fully recover. It is time for a different diagnosis and a different policy prescription.

If my diagnosis is Austrian, my prescription will be for economic liberalism. I will not advise central bankers on the best monetary policy or suggest a formula for risk-based insurance premia on bank deposits. I will instead prescribe a 'constitutional turn' in economic policy to bring us greater economic liberalism. This is the ancient prescription of David Hume and Adam Smith for stable and secure property rights, for good systems of justice and for the 'rule of law'. Only these measures can establish the sort of certainty that promotes human welfare. It is not the certainty of knowing whether people will buy your product; it is the certainty of knowing that if you invest millions or billions, in 50 years the business will be the property of you, your heirs, or those to whom it was freely sold. It is the sort of certainty that enables business planning and investment.

2 HOW THE ECONOMY WENT WRONG

Before prescribing therapy for the economy, we need to understand how things went wrong in the first place: diagnosis precedes therapy. My interpretation of the Great Recession and slow recovery could be described as 'Austrian.' However, at least one prominent economist who would not be considered an Austrian, John Taylor, tells a similar tale. And one economist who might be considered 'Keynesian' has described his interpretation as 'more Keynesian than Monetarist and ... more Austrian than Keynesian' (Leijonhufvud 2009: 749). Thus, my interpretation is not new or original and it is influenced by interpretations given by many others including Leijonhufvud (2008), L. White (2008a, 2009), W. White (2013), Horwitz and Boettke (2009), O'Driscoll (2009), Tayor (2009), and Ravier and Lewin (2012).[1] Young (2009) deserves special mention for an econometric analysis that seems to support an 'Austrian' interpretation of the Great Recession.

---

1   Taylor's semi-popular discussion includes citations to more technical treatments by himself and others. I will not attempt to sort out or indicate where I agree with and where I disagree with Taylor, White, and Horwitz and Boettke. Nor will I try to work out where their different accounts converge and where they diverge.

The story comes in three acts: boom, bust and slump.

Boom

The unsustainable boom came at the end of the 'Great Moderation'. From about 1984 to 2007 the US economy enjoyed unusual stability. Growth was strong and steady and recessions few and mild compared with earlier decades. Citing earlier work, Stock and Watson (2003) coined the term 'Great Moderation' for this period of low volatility in the US economy. As they note, 'the decrease in volatility is not unique to the United States. The relative standard deviation of industrial production indexes for several other developed countries were low in the 1990s' (Stock & Watson 2003: 169). More or less all of the richest countries participated in the Great Moderation (Giannone et al. 2008; Davis & Kahn 2008).

Before the crisis some important economists took much of the credit for the benefits of the Great Moderation. In a 2004 talk that popularised the term, Ben Bernanke said: 'improved monetary policy has likely made an important contribution not only to the reduced volatility of inflation (which is not particularly controversial) but to the reduced volatility of output as well' (Bernanke 2004).

Taylor rules, okay – but not necessarily ideal

The 'Taylor rule' seems to describe the 'improved monetary policy' Bernanke spoke of. Stanford economist John Taylor proposed a simple rule for US monetary policy (Taylor

1993: 202). Taylor advised the Fed to print money when inflation was low and output low relative to potential, and to tap on the monetary brakes when they are high. And because his advice came in the form of a simple equation with specific coefficients, he gave practical advice on how to manage the trade-off between fighting inflation and unemployment.[2]

The rule advised the Fed to target the short-term interest rate (the federal funds rate). This rate 'should be one-and-a-half times the inflation rate plus one-half times the GDP gap plus one' (Taylor 2009, location 519). In this case, the 'GDP gap' is just 'the percent deviation of real GDP from a target', which he takes to be the trend of 2.2 per cent per year growth that held between 1984 and 1992 (Taylor 1993: 202).

It may not be obvious why a rule about *interest rates* is a rule for *monetary policy*. Money and credit are not the same thing (Greenfield and Yeager 1982). They are connected, however. The Taylor rule says how to target the federal funds rate, which is the overnight rate banks charge one another. The Fed buys short-term government bonds called T-bills to lower the federal funds rate. This increase in demand raises the price of the bonds and thus lowers their yield, which gives us a lower short-term interest rate. It also injects money into the economy (you can see why it injects money if you pretend that the Fed pays in cash

---

2   The existence of such a trade-off in the long run is, of course, controversial. But it does exist in the short run whether or not in a form that central banks can reliably exploit.

that it prints to make the purchase – it does the electronic equivalent of that). The Fed sells T-bills to increase the federal funds rate. This increase in supply lowers the price of the bonds and thus raises their yield, which gives us a higher short-term interest rate. It also withdraws money from the economy. Thus, the way central banks interact with the economy creates a connection – or, perhaps, a confusion – between money and credit.

The Taylor rule was based on a lot of research on how different monetary policies seemed to perform. Taylor thought it was about the best practical, actionable rule you could have, at least for the modern US economy. There were theoretically better rules, but they depended on variables such as expected inflation that are hard to measure. With Taylor's simple equation, the Fed could know whether it was following the rule or not. Taylor found it 'perhaps surprising' that the rule fitted Fed practice from 1987 to 1992 rather well. More surprising still, the Federal Reserve seemed to follow the Taylor rule afterwards. It seemed almost as if the experts at the Fed read Taylor's article and got the message. Indeed, transcripts seem to show that monetary policy was self-consciously influenced by the Taylor rule by 1995 if not earlier (Asso et al. 2010). It seems that Janet Yellen was particularly important in bringing about this result (Asso et al. 2010: 2, 15).

The Taylor rule is likely to have contributed to the Great Moderation. Later I will explain why I think any policy rule has important limits and why, therefore, a monetary constitution is preferable. Nevertheless, Taylor's suggestion is more than reasonable for a central bank with the power to conduct monetary policy. Cleaving fast to the Taylor rule prevents strong swings in monetary policy, and moderate monetary policy contributed to the economic stability of the Great Moderation. Other countries seemed to follow a similar monetary policy during the Great Moderation, which may help to explain why the Great Moderation was an international phenomenon (Davis and Kahn 2008; Giannone et al. 2008).

Selgin et al. (2010) note that 'Most authorities do attribute the substantial decline in both the mean rate of inflation and in inflation volatility [in the US] since the early 1980s to improved monetary policy' at the Fed (p. 16). They give reasons to doubt, however, whether this improved monetary policy reflects greater knowledge or wisdom of the monetary authorities in the US. Alternatively, it could be argued, fortuitous real factors lowered the cost of sound monetary policy. Feedback between real and monetary factors makes it hard to decide how much credit to give the authorities for the relatively good monetary policy of the Great Moderation. In any event, two facts remain. Firstly, the policy was relatively good in the period. Secondly, as I will now discuss, the authorities subsequently deviated needlessly from the Taylor rule and thereby brought on the boom and the bust.

From the Taylor rule to the 'loose suit'

The Federal Reserve seems to have followed the Taylor rule until 2002. From early 2002 to late in 2006, however, the Federal Reserve deviated from the Taylor rule by keeping

Figure 5   **Actual federal funds rate versus fed funds rate implied by Taylor rule**

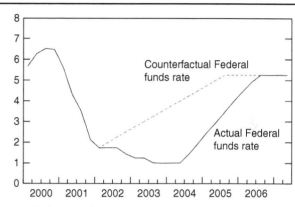

Source: Taylor (2007: 467).

interest rates too low relative to the level the rule would have implied (see Figure 5). A graph in *The Economist* dubs this deviation from the Taylor rule 'loose fitting' monetary policy (unattributed 2007). For the convenience of a label I will call it the 'loose suit'. Unfortunately, as Ahrend (2010) shows, OECD central banks, including the European Central Bank tended to follow a similar loose monetary policy at about the same time although the UK monetary policy was not loose in this period (see Ahrend 2010: 132–36; Benati 2008: 20, 22).

Taylor (2009), White (2009) and others have viewed the loose suit policy as large enough to explain the boom and why it had to end in a bust. Taylor (2009) says, 'The deviation of monetary policy from the Taylor rule was unusually large; no greater or more persistent deviation of actual Fed policy had been seen since the turbulent days of the 1970s. This is clear evidence of monetary excess during the period leading up to the housing boom'. White says the loose suit produced 'a major amplification of cheap credit' (2009: 118).

From a broadly Austrian perspective, the problem with the loose suit was not that it produced an excessive money stock or even rapid growth in the money supply. The questions are whether a loose monetary policy caused an 'artificial' injection of credit and whether that injection of credit drove interest rates below the equilibrium levels they would otherwise have reached. In other words, did monetary expansion send out the false signal that credit was cheap and abundant? The Taylor rule seems well crafted to address such questions. The situation is less clear if we look only at monetary aggregates.

Horwitz and Boettke (2009) say, 'One common measure of the money supply grew by 32.5%'. They refer to M2, which grew by about 33 per cent in the five years from the beginning of 2002 to the end of 2006.[3] This *expansion* of M2 might be compared with a 33 per cent *contraction* in M2 that initiated the Great Depression. The 33 per cent contraction of M2 during the 'Great Contraction', the four years from August 1929 to March 1933 (Friedman & Schwartz 1963: 301–2), was somewhat more abrupt. And equivalent declines in the stock of money are more dangerous than

3 Horwitz and Boettke (2009) used seasonally adjusted M2. My calculations of M2 growth rates use data from the Federal Reserve Bank of St. Louis FRED database, 'M2 Money Stock (M2), Billions of Dollars, Weekly, Seasonally Adjusted', http://research.stlouisfed.org/fred2

increases. The comparison may nevertheless seem to suggest that the monetary expansion of 2002–6 was large and portentous. However, Henderson and Hummel (2008) have noted that monetary aggregates were growing at similar rates both before and during the loose suit. The M2 money supply grew by about 42 per cent, for example, from 1997 to 2001, or by about 10 per cent *more* than from 2002 to 2006. It grew by about 36 per cent in the period 2007–11. But, as George Selgin (2008) has noted in his response to Henderson and Hummel: 'one cannot accurately gauge the easiness of monetary policy by looking at money stock measures alone. Instead, one must look at measures that indicate the relationship between the stock of money on one hand and the real demand for it or, if one prefers, its velocity.' Selgin thinks the money supply was expanding more rapidly than money demand in the period of the loose suit, and he may be right given factors such as the discouragement to money holding created by asset-price inflation. While it is dangerous to draw inferences from money growth rates alone, the Taylor rule seems to give us reliable evidence of credit expansion and 'artificially' low interest rates in the loose suit period.

Jordà et al. (2011) support the view that excess credit, not excess money, can produce a large financial crisis. They reviewed financial crises in developed economies over the 140-year period from 1870 to 2008. They find: 'The global crises of 1873, 1890 1907, 1930/31, and 2007/08 were ... preceded by periods in which interest rates were unusually low relative to the real growth rate of the economy' (pp. 352–53). They also find: 'Both national and global crises are preceded by an expansion in money and credit. But the expansion of bank loans is more pronounced, suggesting that credit, not money is the key variable' (pp. 354–55). These findings seem to support a broadly 'Austrian' theory of business cycles, as least when applied to global financial crises.

Taylor (2009), White (2009) and Horwitz and Boettke (2009) agree that a disproportionate fraction of the false credit created by the loose suit ended up in the housing market. Taylor notes that housing price inflation jumped sharply in 2003. According to one popular measure of housing prices, the Case–Shiller 'Composite-10' index, housing prices had been rising without interruption since March 1996. Some of this growth was steep enough to suggest a bubble. It peaked at 14.5 per cent per year in January 2001. Thereafter, the growth in house prices continued at a more moderate pace until it started to accelerate again in May 2002. The annual rate of increase in housing prices hit an astonishing 20.5 per cent in July of 2004, after which housing prices rose more slowly until price changes finally turned negative in January of 2007.[4]

The timing of the resurgence in the growth of housing prices beginning in 2002 has suggested to many observers that the loose suit rejuvenated the housing bubble. Taylor (2009) attributes much of the excess risk taking in the housing market to the low interest rates of the loose suit.

---

4   The Case–Shiller numbers can be found at http://www.standard andpoors.com/indices/articles/en/us/?articleType=XLS&assetID =1221192472066

He says: 'there is an interaction between the monetary excesses and the risk-taking excesses' in the housing sector. White (2009: 115) says, the 'Federal Reserve's expansionary monetary policy supplied the means for unsustainable housing prices and unsustainable mortgage financing.' Horwitz and Boettke (2009) say the loose suit gave the housing industry 'a giant green light to expand.'

The facts reviewed so far do not explain why the loose suit gave us a renewed housing boom rather than some more diffused consequences. The key point is that low interest rates give a disproportionate stimulus to the most interest-sensitive sectors such as manufacturing and construction (Carlino and Defina 1998: 572–73). Housing was not the only interest-sensitive sector to respond to the loose suit. For example, the value of capital goods (excluding defence and aircraft) had been declining since the autumn of 2000, hitting a low in April 2003, when, in response to the loose suit presumably, they started to rise sharply. They rose 30.6 per cent from April 2003 to April 2007, which implies a continuous annual rate of increase of 6.7 per cent.[5] The work of Young (2009) takes a different approach but also comes up with conclusions that suggest that sectors that were more interest sensitive expanded relative to sectors that were less interest sensitive before the Great Recession.

---

5   Author's calculations from the Federal Reserve Bank of St. Louis FRED database, Series ANXAVS, Value of Manufacturers' Shipments for Capital Goods: Nondefense Capital Goods Excluding Aircraft Industries (http://research.stlouisfed.org/fred2/graph/?id =ANXAVS).

The loose suit gave all the interest-sensitive sectors a push. Housing got an extra push because of measures of the federal government touted as promoting home ownership. In particular, as White (2008a, 2009), Taylor (2009) and Horwitz and Boettke (2009) all note, the government-sponsored enterprises Fannie Mae and Freddie Mac actively purchased mortgage-backed securities. The housing sector was politicised as suggested by the discovery that Freddie Mac was making illegal campaign contributions from 2000 to 2003 (unattributed 2006). Securitised mortgages helped to feed the demand coming from Fannie Mae and Freddie Mac. Jones (2000) explains how securitisation allows banks to wiggle out of capital requirements imposed by government regulators without unloading much portfolio risk onto third parties. The strategies Jones explained might have been less effective if the financial rating agencies had been more conservative. Levy and Peart (2008) and Levy (2009) explain the sense in which the rating agencies are creations of the government and why they had an incentive to produce unrealistically optimistic ratings. Finally, the failure of the rating agencies would have been less important if there had been no presumption that the government would bail out the larger financial firms.

Thus, several complementary government failures contributed to concentrate expansion disproportionately in the housing sector and create excess risk taking in financial markets. The central underlying fact, however, was the loose suit and not housing policy, too-big-to-fail, securitisation, credit default swaps, other fancy financial instruments, or the failure of the rating agencies.

Deregulation and the financial crisis

Deregulation was not a cause of the crisis. Horwitz and Boettke (2009) say that it was a myth that there was deregulation in the period of the boom or prior to it. There have been many changes in financial market regulation over the years. Some of these changes might count as 'deregulation'. Krugman (2012: 61) mentions three Congressional Acts in particular. The Monetary Control Act of 1980 relaxed restrictions on the interest rates banks could offer depositors. The Garn–St. Germain Act of 1982 relaxed certain restrictions on savings and loans and allowed commercial banks to offer adjustable-rate mortgages. The Gramm–Leach–Bliley Act of 1999 reversed a provision of the Glass–Steagall Act of 1933 to the effect that investment banking, commercial banking and insurance must be segregated. Gramm–Leach–Bliley is sometimes called the 'repeal' of Glass–Steagall, but the 1933 Act had several important provisions, including the creation of the Federal Deposit Insurance Corporation (FDIC), that were not reversed by Gramm–Leach–Bliley. There are at least two problems with using this or any similar list to show that we had deregulation of the financial markets.

Firstly, only the last item, which is probably the most salient example of a supposed deregulation, is close in time to the onset of the boom: and it is not very close in time. Meltzer (2009: 27) says: 'I would challenge anybody to point to something important that was deregulated during the last eight years. Nothing much was deregulated. The last major financial deregulation was the 1999 act that President Clinton signed, removing the Glass–Steagall provisions separating commercial and investment banking'. Meltzer also points to the lack of evidence that the mixing of commercial and investment banking contributed in any way to the Great Depression (Meltzer 2009: 27–28).

Furthermore, the great thicket of regulations and controls was never lifted from financial markets. The regulatory changes cited as 'deregulation' left in place the FDIC, deposit insurance and more or less all the previous regulatory apparatus. Nor did such measures prevent the further regulatory acts that followed. Even within each act we can find measures that do not look much like 'deregulation'. The Monetary Control Act of 1980 expanded Fed control of depository institutions and more than doubled the value of deposits guaranteed by the FDIC. The Garn–St. Germain Act included new authorisation permitting the FDIC to buy up assets of troubled banks, make deposits with them or buy their securities, and make such institutions or their corporate owners guarantee against losses. Finally, the 'repeal' of Glass–Steagall may have been a sop to Citigroup, which was created when Citibank and Travelers merged in 1998. The merger would have put Citigroup at odds with Glass–Steagall after a two-year grace period expired. Rather than divesting itself of some of its holdings, however, Citigroup lobbied for a change in the law. Gramm–Leach–Bliley was the result (see Suellentrop 2002; Broome and Markham n.d.). One observer said of Gramm–Leach–Bliley, 'Citigroup is not the result of that act but the cause of it' (Thomas 2002). In some circles, it seems, the Act was known as the 'Citigroup Relief Act' (Broome and Markham n.d.: 1). Thus, the most salient act of 'deregulation' in this period may be more crony capitalism than laissez-faire.

The central fact behind the Great Recession, then, was not 'deregulation'; nor was it, as I have said, housing policy, derivatives or even too-big-to-fail. The loose suit was the central fact creating the boom and ensuring the subsequent bust. Without monetary expansion, all the other infirmities of the system, though harmful separately and together, could not have produced a boom–bust cycle.

Bust

Monetary mistakes cause a real misallocation of resources

As we have seen, the loose suit was both a monetary injection and a credit injection. But the injected credit, like the injected money, was conjured from thin air. It represented no change in underlying scarcities. The low interest rate encouraged more borrowing, but not more saving. To investors it seems as if the people had become more like the ant, who works hard and saves for the coming winter. By lowering the return to thrift, however, the loose suit made the people behave more like the grasshopper, who plays today and gives no thought to the coming winter. Horwitz and Boettke (2009) explain: 'Fed policy gave the would-be suppliers of capital – those who might have been tempted to save – a giant red light. With rates so low, they had no incentive to put their money in the bank for others to borrow.'

The loose suit gave entrepreneurs in interest-sensitive sectors a false signal that resources for their activities had grown more abundant while at the same time reducing the return to thrift for consumers. In effect, the system is giving signals to people to consume more and invest more too (Garrison (2001) clarifies this important aspect of Austrian business cycle theory). But there is a trade-off between consumption and investment. If we are going to build more houses, the labour and other factors of production to make them must be drawn away from other goods. But the low interest rates of the loose suit told consumers to continue buying consumer goods while also telling businesses to invest. At the same time, the saving necessary to finance the investment did not exist – consumers were not decreasing consumption.

Something had to give. The turning point in the Great Recession was a decline in housing prices. The financial sector had been taking on too much risk, in part because of too-big-to-fail. Thus, when housing prices started to fall and mortgagees to fail, the whole thing unravelled.[6] Taylor (2009) discusses how falling house prices encouraged mortgage delinquency: 'When [house] prices are falling, the incentives to make payments are much less and turn negative if the price of the house falls below the value of the mortgage. Hence, delinquencies and foreclosures rise.' And, of course, as housing prices and general economic conditions both decline, it becomes harder to avoid delinquency even for many households determined to avoid it if at all possible.

6   On 6 October 2008 the Fed began to pay interest on both required and excess reserves. This new policy may have made the crisis worse by causing money multipliers to fall and by discouraging lending by banks. I am not aware of any unambiguous empirical evidence on these points, however.

The special circumstances leading up to the Great Recession ensured that the turning point would be triggered by a decline in housing prices, and that this turn would eventually produce a financial crisis. Even without those special circumstances, however, a failure in some sector and subsequent recession had to follow from the false boom created by monetary expansion. Stimulating both consumption and interest-sensitive sectors creates inconsistencies in the plans of investors and households, and those inconsistencies are exposed in the inevitable bust.[7]

The trigger for an Austrian crisis could be a real factor or a monetary factor. In practice, the real and monetary factors go together, and it can be hard to decide which came first in a given bust. It may be worth considering how each sort of factor works to ensure an end to the boom.

Real factors alone would eventually precipitate a bust even if monetary factors were somehow kept in abeyance. The expansion in the interest-sensitive sectors does not

---

7 My exposition has followed the 'Austrian' theory of the trade cycle, the canonical expression of which is probably Hayek (1935, [1967]). It would be easy to exaggerate the difference between Austrian and monetarist models of the trade cycle, however, as illustrated by Steve Horwitz's (2000) skilful blending of the two. In terms of Fisher's (1933) analysis, monetary expansion creates both 'debt disease' and 'dollar disease'. It creates a debt disease by injecting false credit into the system. It creates a dollar disease because, in the absence of hyperinflation, the monetary expansion must eventually slow down relative to expectations, creating a liquidity crisis. Fisher says, 'It is the combination of both – the debt disease coming first, then precipitating the dollar disease – which works the greatest havoc' (1933: 344).

correspond to any desired reduction in current consumption. This disconnect between consumption and investment creates plans to use more real resources than are available. There may not be enough timber, for example, to allow everyone's plans to succeed. There is not enough timber to make all the kitchen tables (consumption goods) being ordered *and* all the houses (investment goods) being ordered. The lack of timber will manifest itself as a price spike. Developers find they cannot afford to buy the timber needed to finish the houses they have started and go bankrupt, putting construction workers out of their jobs and precipitating the crisis. Once the bust arrives we can no longer imagine the monetary factors to be in abeyance. The increased rate of loan defaults in interest-sensitive sectors will force up bank reserve ratios and cause a relative contraction of the money supply.

Monetary factors alone would also eventually precipitate a bust even if real factors were somehow kept in abeyance. At some point there must be a reduction of the money supply relative to trend (Hayek 1933 [1975]: 176) or there will be hyperinflation.[8] As new money is injected into the economy, prices rise, which reduces the purchasing power of each existing pound or dollar. The effects of this price inflation are like a reduction in the money supply. Continued monetary expansion can offset the deflationary effects of

---

8   The relevant trend is defined by the expectations of the public. The trend will have one definition under the assumption of adaptive expectations, another under the assumption of rational expectations, and so on.

price inflation, but only if the quantities of money injected each period rise exponentially. The same percentage increase corresponds to an exponentially growing increase in the number of pounds or dollars added to the system. Even this expanding expansion is unlikely to be sufficient to hold off the deflationary consequences of price inflation. When the public comes to expect price inflation the same percentage increase in the money supply will more quickly produce the expected increase in prices, wiping out the expansionary effect of the new money. The money supply must be increased at an increasing rate, resulting eventually in hyperinflation and the collapse of the currency. Thus, the process simply cannot continue indefinitely. Unless the currency collapses from hyperinflation, there must come a time at which the money supply falls relative to trend (Hayek 1934: 159–62).[9] But the reduction in the money supply relative to trend has deflationary consequences; it brings on the bust. Once the bust arrives we can no longer imagine the real factors to be in abeyance. The contraction of the money supply relative to trend, if not in absolute, will cause a reduction in credit below the level needed to keep firms in interest-sensitive sectors afloat.

---

9   The institutional context for the Austrian theory of the trade cycle as discussed in Hayek (1933 [1976], 1934, 1935 [1967]) is a gold standard with a central bank. The currency in such an environment is like a rubber band: if it is stretched, it will snap back. In such an environment, crises will typically begin with monetary contraction. What separates the Austrian from the monetarist explanation is the claim that such a contraction may often be the necessary consequence of a prior expansion of money and credit.

The loss of credit ensures an increase in the rate of bankruptcies and in the rate of unemployment.

Other Austrian explanations of the crisis

Other economists have articulated a broadly Austrian theory of the business cycle. I noted above the evidence given by Jordà et al. (2011). In the wake of the 'tech boom' and subsequent recession of 2001, several economists began to warn of distortions that are not reflected in price inflation. Borio and Lowe (2002: 27) warn that 'financial imbalances can build up in low inflation environments' and that 'Monetary policy rules that do not take these imbalances into account may unwittingly accommodate their further build up.' They add the prescient comment: 'Against this background, there is a risk of greater amplitude in financial cycles going hand in hand with more disruptive booms and busts in real economic activity.' They explicitly link their concern with financial imbalances signalling distortions in the real economy with the Austrian school and contrast such concerns with those macroeconomic models which imply that 'responding to inflation will, over time, guarantee appropriate macroeconomic outcomes.' White (2013) gives an explicitly Austrian interpretation of the Great Recession. He argues that, viewed from an Austrian perspective, the broadly Keynesian policy followed over recent decades has been an 'error'. He says, 'Below the surface of the Great Moderation, such policies encouraged financial exuberance which allowed significant "malinvestments" to build up in both phases of successive credit cycles' (p. 20).

Why is there unemployment in the 'bust' phase?

The Great Recession has brought the Austrian theory of the trade cycle to the attention of the financial press as well. Martin Wolf (2010) of the *Financial Times*, for example, expresses sympathy for Austrian explanations. However, Wolf's qualified praise for Austrian ideas caused Paul Krugman (2010) to repeat a criticism of the theory that has been raised by others as well. If unemployment in the slump 'results from the difficulty of "adaptation of the structure of production"' then 'Why isn't there similar unemployment during the boom, as workers are transferred into investment goods production?'

This raises an interesting challenge to Austrian explanations of the boom and bust and seems to have created considerable perplexity among defenders and critics alike (see Bresciani-Turroni 1936: 175–76; Haberler 1938: 67; Hummel 1979; Tullock 1988; Evans 2010) and yet its resolution is straightforward. The boom creates an overall increase in the demand for labour; the bust creates an overall decrease in demand for labour: if wages are sticky, there will be a period of unemployment. The bust also leads to a reduction in credit, which is a factor of production that is complementary to labour in all its applications. In the long run these problems can be overcome as producers adopt to the new situation and prices and wages adjust;

however, adjustment will not be immediate. There are a variety of explanations for slow adjustment that might be applicable to the bust stage of an Austrian cycle, including sticky wages, sticky information (Mankiw and Reis 2002), and search costs. The increase in unemployment should reverse in the medium term, however, unless other serious policy errors are made.[10] Experience seems to show that adjustments can be slow in labour markets, particularly in response to a large shock.[11]

I will address one important example, uncertainty, below in my 'equilibrium theory of the state of confidence'. To anticipate this, the bust will create a higher than expected rate of loan defaults, causing an increase in the costs of financial intermediation and, therefore, a lower state of confidence. This 'real' factor cannot be avoided once the bust hits and is also a sufficient explanation of 'asymmetry'.

---

10 The question of why there must be unemployment in the bust phase of an Austrian crisis is different from the question of why there was *persistent high* unemployment in a given historical episode. Higgs (1997) blames the persistence of unemployment of the Great Depression in part on regime uncertainty, which is by no means a necessary consequence of an Austrian cycle.

11 Experts in monetary theory might also recognise that the boom might be characterised by an excess supply of money and (therefore) an excess demand for goods, while the bust will necessarily be characterised by an excess demand for money and (therefore) an excess supply of goods. From this monetary perspective, the high employment of the boom and the unemployment of the bust reflect a rather neat symmetry in Austrian business cycle theory.

Slump

Recovery from the bust has been slow. In the UK, output is still below 2008 levels and well below the levels that would have pertained had there been trend growth since the crash. Indeed, by some measures, the UK has experienced its worst economic performance in its industrial history. In the US, output growth has also been slow compared with growth after other post-war recessions. Robert Hall (2011) has dubbed the slow recovery from the Great Recession the 'long slump'.

The slow pace of recovery requires explanation. Standard neo-classical macroeconomics does not have an adequate explanation. Many economists continue to argue that the problem is a deficiency of 'aggregate demand'. These economists want us to 'stimulate' our way out of the slump. The trouble is that repeated stimulatory measures have not effected a complete recovery. In the UK, for example, heavy government borrowing has led the national debt to double in five years and yet the UK has endured, arguably, the worst slump in its industrial history.

Other economists have made arguments for the continued lack of growth that depend on confidence, uncertainty or both. Taylor (2009) emphasises uncertainty; Akerlof and Shiller (2009) have emphasised confidence. But these considerations had little role to play in the models that dominated macroeconomics until the onset of the crisis. Since the crisis there has been increasing interest in confidence and uncertainty (Baker et al. 2013). Unfortunately, this interest has not yet corresponded to great innovations in macroeconomic theory beyond an increasing attention to 'uncertainty shocks' (see, for example, Bloom 2009; Orlik and Veldkamp 2014). Our understanding of the state of confidence is little or no better now than it was before the onset of the crisis. The Austrian school has concepts and tools to apply. Indeed, Austrian economics points to a true theory of confidence, which can hardly be said to exist elsewhere.[12] The Austrian theory of confidence developed below builds mostly on Higgs (1997) and Koppl (2002). Before developing these ideas, it may be helpful to review how macroeconomic thought went wrong before the crisis and where it seems to be heading now. Without this, we cannot explain the Great Recession.

---

12 Whether there are any rival theories of confidence depends on what counts as a 'theory'. The financial fragility hypothesis of Hyman Minsky (1975, 1982, 1992) does not have a clear mechanism or clear empirical implications. Keynes's (1936) analysis, from which I have borrowed opportunistically, has many virtues. Those virtues do not include testable implications, however, making it doubtful whether he has a 'theory' of confidence.

3 THE DEVELOPMENT OF MACROECONOMICS FROM WORLD WAR II TO THE FINANCIAL CRASH

Post-war hydraulic Keynesianism

Macroeconomics as a field of study was mostly a response to the Great Depression of the 1930s. The catastrophic failure of the economic system seemed to suggest a corresponding failure in economic analysis. Keynes's 1936 book, *The General Theory of Employment, Interest and Money*, pointed to the capitalist system and suggested that it was subject to sudden collapse and chronic under-employment of resources. Declaring it 'a work of genius', Paul Samuelson (1946: 190) famously described the *General Theory* as 'a badly written book' that is 'poorly organized' and 'abounds in mares' nests of confusions.' Nevertheless, Keynes's revolutionary analysis gave rise to macroeconomics as the science of government policy to control employment, interest and inflation.

The difficulty in understanding the *General Theory* may have contributed to its success as the founding text of macroeconomics. The book is open to alternative interpretations. In the post-war years, if you wanted to propose interventionist policies to 'stabilise the economy' or otherwise improve economic performance, you might well cite the *General Theory* as the source or context for your proposed policies. Thus, a variety of interventionist systems of thought were labelled 'Keynesian'.

After the war, one version of economics, described as Keynesian, came to dominate macroeconomics. This breed of Keynesianism would estimate a consumption function, an investment function and other functions intended to represent stable relationships determining the overall levels of output, employment and prices. Changing policy variables such as the government deficit could, it was thought, shift these functions about and give us a better combination of output, employment and prices. Increasing money growth, for example, would inevitably cause some price inflation, but it would also reduce unemployment. This supposed inverse relationship between inflation and unemployment (Samuelson and Solow 1960) is known as the 'Phillips curve'.[1] Assuming a stable Phillips curve, any event that might increase unemployment could be met with a bit of inflation as a reliable offset.

This sort of macroeconomics is sometimes called 'hydraulic Keynesianism'. Keynes was claimed as an important source and it was 'hydraulic' because the models resembled the mathematical description of a plumbing system. The flow of spending in an economy looked like the flow of water in a system of pipes. And just as we can

---

1 This is despite the fact that the relationship originally identified by Phillips (1958) connected unemployment not to overall inflation, but to the growth of money wages.

regulate the flow of water with a few valves, we can regulate the economy with a few relatively simple policy instruments – or so it was thought.

Indeed, W. A. Phillips (of Phillips curve fame) constructed a machine in 1949 in which circulating water represented the flow of spending in the economy, and the various valves, chambers and settings of the device reflected assumptions about the consumption function, the investment function and the like.[2,3] The Phillips machine was an analogue computer relying not on the flow of electrons though copper wire but on the flow of water through a system of sluices and chambers.

Challenges to hydraulic Keynesianism and the development of pre-crisis macroeconomics

Monetarists such as Milton Friedman challenged hydraulic Keynesians on theoretical and empirical grounds. Friedman (1968) and Phelps (1968) argued that the trade-off between inflation and unemployment was temporary. They argued that there is a 'natural' rate of unemployment reflecting 'real' (i.e. non-monetary) factors such as the extent of unionisation, regulation and the time spent searching

---

2 At the time of writing, 'Bill Phillips Moniac Economic Analog Computer', a charming video of the machine in action, can be found on YouTube.

3 Editor's note: the Bank of England's museum also has a similar mechanism, which visitors can try out, with a hot-air balloon purporting to show how changes to monetary policy can keep the economy on track.

for a new job after leaving an old job. The economy tends to hit the natural rate of unemployment no matter what the inflation rate. In the long run, therefore, the Phillips curve is vertical. Friedman and Schwartz (1963) examined American business cycles from 1867 to 1960. They concluded that downturns were preceded and caused by reductions in the rate of money growth, and that such episodes of monetary contraction (relative to trend) were needless policy errors. In particular, the main cause of the Great Depression in America was a policy-induced contraction of the money supply.

The monetarists enjoyed some success in opposing hydraulic Keynesianism. In particular, as Mishkin (2011: 4) points out, almost all economists came to agree with Friedman's famous adage that inflation is always and everywhere a monetary phenomenon (Friedman 1968: 17).

The rational expectations revolution, which led to modern macroeconomics, did further damage to hydraulic Keynesianism. Following Muth (1961), Lucas (1972, 1976) articulated what would become the central feature of modern macroeconomics: expectations are formed as if the representative agent knows the true model, and the 'true' model is whatever the theorist says it is. The limits of rational-expectations modelling probably seem more important today than they did before the financial crisis of 2007 and 2008. At the time of the rational-expectations revolution, however, it offered a valuable correction to the more mechanical sort of macroeconomics that had previously dominated policy.

Lucas (1976) pointed out a problem with hydraulic Keynesianism. The theory assumes that the different functions being estimated would not change when policy changed. But those functions reflected the plans and actions of people who are trying to understand the economy in which they act. For that reason, the functions may not have the sort of stability required for the theory to work. In particular, the public will sooner or later catch on to the link between expansionary monetary policy and inflation rates. When they do, inflation will no longer reduce unemployment. Anticipating increases in inflation, workers may not imagine that their higher wages represent more purchasing power, suppliers may not mistake an increase in output prices for an increase in underlying demand for their goods, and so on. The public will protect itself from the expected inflation, thereby eliminating the supposedly beneficial effects. This criticism of hydraulic Keynesianism is the 'Lucas critique'.

Water in a pipe does not ask what the plumber is doing, but people in a market do ask what the *government* is up to. Hydraulic Keynesians neglected this difference between people and water. They were therefore vulnerable to the Lucas critique, which helped to open the way to neo-classical macroeconomics and 'rational expectations'. As noted above, the assumption of rational expectations says that expectations are formed as if the 'representative agent' knew the true model.

The assumption of rational expectations is not quite the same as an assumption of 'no errors'. Any one buyer or seller may be irrational or may make mistaken calculations.

But, if one person under-estimates the inflation rate, for example, another over-estimates it. On average, the many buyers and sellers, anthropomorphised as the representative agent, expect the inflation rate predicted by the true model of the economy. The inflation rate (or value of other variables) predicted by the economist's model might also be mistaken. But, because the model is right by assumption, the errors it generates could not be avoided. Freakish weather, for example, might destroy this year's crop, driving up the price of corn and everything else. The economist's model will under-estimate inflation that year. But such errors have no systematic component since, by assumption, the economist's model has captured all the systematic elements in the economy. Thus, aggregate errors are zero on average and serially uncorrelated.

Challenges to and developments of pre-crisis macroeconomics

The representative agent of rational expectations models is a curious beast. His behaviour is ultimately derived (in theory) from the behaviour of individuals, but it is not necessarily similar to the behaviour of any individual. Almost anything goes with the representative agent. Kirman's (1992) review of the mathematics of representative agents concludes (p. 134):

> That well-behaved individuals need not produce a well-behaved representative agent; that the reaction of a representative agent to change need not reflect how the

individuals of the economy would respond to change; [and] that the preferences of a representative agent over choices may be diametrically opposed to those of society as a whole.

Kirman (2009) says: 'to assume that behavior at one level can be assimilated to that at the other is simply erroneous' (p. 11). This situation seems hard to accept even if we ignore all the differences between real people and the rational agents of standard microeconomic theory.

Given that the representative agent can be so different from the agents it is supposed to represent, one might wonder why all macroeconomists do not agree with Kirman that 'the representative agent should have no future' (1992: 134). The macroeconomic emperor has no clothes, and yet macroeconomists have simply assumed that the representative agent is well behaved and continued to theorise using the concept. In principle, observation could justify the assumption that the representative agent is well behaved and thus similar to individual decision makers. In practice, however, the available data do not support any such conclusion. They are ambiguous at best. The use of representative-agent models seems to owe more to the habits of macroeconomists, and perhaps their interests, than to logic, principle or fact.

The new classical economics of the 1970s, which initially dominated rational expectations models, had two important implications. Firstly, the ideas suggested that any attempt by policymakers to systematically fool rational economic agents in order to cause the economy to deviate from equilibrium will be unsuccessful. Among other things, this fact renders active monetary policy ineffective (Sargent and Wallace 1975, 1976). Secondly, we had the Lucas critique. This was the idea that relationships estimated for a given period depend on the particular policy regime in place and that parameters should not be assumed to hold steady when policies underlying the original estimation change (Lucas 1976).

During the 1980s rational expectations models came increasingly to fall into one of two groups: real business cycle (RBC) theory and new-Keynesian economics. Articles by Kydland and Prescott (1982) and Long and Plosser (1983) helped launch RBC theory. Mankiw and Romer (1991) collected the lead articles in new-Keynesian economics.

Real business cycle models

RBC theories assume the classical dichotomy. That is, they assume that changes in nominal variables have no relevant effect on changes in real variables. An increase in the money supply, for example, may double the price of both apples and oranges but will not change the relative prices of different goods and services. RBC theories also assume the macroeconomic irrelevance of market imperfections. These two assumptions take monetary surprises off the table as explanations of booms and busts. The central bank cannot surprise the representative agent with an unexpectedly high or low rate of inflation because the central bank and the public are using the same model of the economy and, therefore, of how the central bank should behave. If the central bank tries to create inflation, it will not be a surprise to economic agents and so they will adjust their behaviour in anticipation of the change.

The assumptions underlying RBC models are certainly questionable. If you assume perfect markets and the classical dichotomy, you cannot explain booms, busts and recessions with monetary factors. For example, you cannot blame the central bank for contracting the money supply and creating, thereby, an excess demand for money with its corresponding excess supply of goods. All prices will just adjust simultaneously. In RBC models, money is less than a veil because is it perfectly transparent and it never flutters (George Selgin entitled his 1997 collection of essays by Leland Yeager *The Fluttering Veil*). Given this, real factors are necessary to explain recessions, such as a change in technology or resource availability. The importance of RBC theory is reflected in the comment of Nelson and Plosser (1982: 141), who say: 'stochastic variation due to real factors is an essential element of any model of macroeconomic fluctuation'.

Kydland and Prescott (1982) built an RBC model in which economic ups and downs are driven by abrupt changes ('shocks') in technology. They then found a set of numerical values for the variables in the model such that the behaviour of the imaginary model economy seemed close to the recorded behaviour of US data from the period 1950–79.

This method of calibrating the model follows Lucas's (1977: 11) advice to construct 'a model in the most literal sense: a fully articulated artificial economy which behaves through time so as to imitate closely the time series behavior of actual economies'. Similarly, Lucas (1980) says: 'One of the functions of theoretical economics is to provide fully articulated, artificial economic systems that can serve as laboratories in which policies that would be prohibitively expensive to experiment with in actual economies can be tested out at much lower cost.'

Kydland and Prescott (1982) and Long and Plosser (1983) were particularly important in transforming the rational expectations revolution into the rigid orthodoxy of dynamic stochastic general equilibrium (DSGE) models. DSGE models are *dynamic* because they describe the behaviour of an imaginary economy over time. They are *stochastic* because some of the key variables of the model such as productivity and labour supply are subject to random shocks. Finally, they are *general equilibrium* models because all markets are considered at once.

DSGE models are sometimes described as 'toy economies' to underline how much they simplify real economies. A modern economy has many people and many goods, each different from the others. It changes continuously with innovations and surprises at every turn. DSGE models boil all this diversity down to a few equations representing, typically, one person, the representative individual, choosing how to distribute one good, labelled 'consumption', over time given a production technology that can change only when a random shock alters one or more coefficients of the equation linking a few inputs to the output of the one consumption good. Even the more elaborate DSGE models such as the important model of Smets and Wouters (2003) do not exceed about 30 equations.

Since the original Kydland and Prescott paper, the RBC literature has expanded rapidly. King and Rebelo (2000) provide an overview. For example, Cole and Ohanian (1999, 2000, 2004), Cole et al. (2005) and Ohanian (2009) analyse the Great Depression and New Deal era as real phenomena. In addition to historical studies, many RBC theorists use the DSGE framework to derive policy recommendations. Chari and Kehoe (1999) review the RBC literature on optimal fiscal and monetary policy.

New Keynesian theory

New Keynesian theory is the main rival to RBC within standard macroeconomics. New Keynesian economics rejects both the classical dichotomy and the assumption of perfect markets (Mankiw and Romer 1991: 2). New Keynesian models assume certain imperfections and model them explicitly. Those imperfections, such as sticky wages, allow policy – especially monetary policy – to influence output, employment and prices. For New Keynesians, unlike RBC theorists, 'market imperfections in the economy are crucial for understanding economic fluctuations' (Mankiw and Romer 1991: 2).

The frictions of New Keynesian macroeconomics are theoretically justified by an earlier literature showing that wages and prices are sticky and thus somewhat slow to adjust to changes in supply and demand (see Mankiw 1985; Akerlof and Yellen 1986). Of course, these sticky prices must have a cause. That cause might be wage contracts that can be revised only at periodic intervals or 'menu costs' – that is, the time and expense of issuing a new set of prices.

Building on Calvo (1983), Rotemberg and Woodford (1997: 299) were the first to incorporate 'impediments to the free adjustment of prices' into a DSGE model. They simulate outcomes under various hypothetical monetary policy rules. Since DSGE models have microeconomic foundations, they are thought to be capable of making welfare comparisons of the representative agents to determine the utility-maximising monetary rule. In particular, monetary policy can aim at too much price stability, which limits the economy's ability to promptly adapt to changes in technology and resource availability. However, Kirman (1992, 2009) challenges such welfare comparisons on the grounds that the preferences of the representative individual may not be representative of any particular individual. Indeed, as we have seen, 'the preferences of a representative agent over choices may be diametrically opposed to those of society as a whole' (Kirman 1992: 134). Nevertheless, the idea that monetary shocks could have real implications returned to macroeconomic theory with the advent of New Keynesian models.

It became the norm for central banks and others to evaluate monetary policy rules within a DSGE framework and Clarida et al. (1999) provide a survey of the early literature. Erceg et al. (2000: 305–6) add wage rigidities to the standard sticky price model. They note that including both 'makes a critical difference' because the economy will not move to the best theoretical equilibrium (the 'Pareto optimum,' in which any further adjustment would be bad for someone) unless wages, prices or both are completely flexible. Mankiw and Reis (2002, 2007) suggest replacing the sticky price assumption with 'sticky information' whereby prices adjust slowly because it takes time for the relevant information to work its way through the economy. Since some agents base decisions on outdated information, the dynamic response 'resembles Phillips curves with backward-looking expectations' (Mankiw and Reis 2002: 1296). More recently, Christiano et al. (2005: 2) show that only 'moderate degrees of nominal rigidities' are necessary to 'generate inertial inflation and persistent output movements in response to a monetary policy shock'.

Where are we now?

Although a consensus has yet to emerge with respect to which rigidities (if any) to include, there has been a strong convergence on DSGE modelling. At about the time the financial crisis became acute in late 2008, Chari et al. (2008) published an NBER working paper celebrating convergence on DSGE models. The abstract says: 'Macroeconomists have largely converged on method, model design, reduced-form shocks, and principles of policy advice.' The article is mostly a criticism of some strands of DSGE in favour of others. In making their argument, however, they emphasise the hegemony of DSGE models. 'This type of model,' they say, 'can be so generally defined that it incorporates all types of frictions.' Indeed, the paper suggests that the authors cannot imagine substantive criticisms of DSGE.

DSGE dominates macroeconomics, but not everyone is on board. As we have already noted, Kirman (2009) rejects representative agent models. He argues forcefully that DSGE cannot adequately represent the Great Recession. For Kirman, 'the crisis is a story of contagion, of interdependence, interaction, networks and trust. Yet these notions do not figure prominently in modern macroeconomic models' (p. 3). As we shall see, contagion, networks and connectivity are important to the new trends emerging in macroeconomics. These new trends started before the crisis, but seem to have obtained most of their momentum from the crisis.

At least one prominent New Keynesian has lamented the state of modern macroeconomics. Mankiw (2006: 39) says that neo-classical macroeconomics is 'too abstract and insufficiently practical.' He claims 'macroeconomic research of the past three decades has had only minor impact on the practical analysis of monetary or fiscal policy' (p. 42). He describes the past several decades as 'an unfortunate wrong turn,' but he still does not openly endorse abandoning DSGE (Mankiw 2006: 44).

Against such attacks, Woodford (2009) defends neo-classical macroeconomics. He argues that the Fed has 'incorporated many insights from the research literature of the 1970s and 1980s' into their primary policy model (p. 276). Woodford expresses contentment when saying that 'there are no longer such fundamental disagreements among leading macroeconomists about what kind of questions one might reasonably seek to answer, or what kinds of theoretical analyses or empirical studies should be admitted as contributions to knowledge' (2009: 268).

Woodford's remark may have been rash. Shortly before the 'marginalist revolution' radically transformed value theory in economics, John Stuart Mill said: 'Happily, there is nothing in the laws of value which remains for the present or any future writer to clear up; the theory of the subject is complete' (Mill 1948: III.1.ii). Current trends in macroeconomics suggest that Woodford's sanguine defence of neo-classical and New Keynesian models may prove as misplaced as Mill's sanguine defence of classical value theory.

4 SOME STRANDS OF NEW THINKING IN FINANCE AND MACROECONOMICS

Despite the convergence of views among mainstream economists, since the financial crisis there have been more voices raised in opposition to the consensus. The crisis has put DSGE models somewhat on the defensive. It is hard to guess whether DSGE models will be driven into a minority position in macroeconomics or retain something at least close to their recent hegemony. Current trends suggest, however, that mainstream macroeconomics will come to include an increasing number of models that represent, in one way or another, bounded rationality, radical uncertainty, animal spirits and complexity dynamics. These ideas are not necessarily new. However, they have not so far been widely accommodated into the mainstream of thinking among practitioners and theoreticians working in macroeconomics and analysing financial markets.

Unfortunately, most work of this type supports an interventionist approach to monetary policy and the regulation of financial markets. For this reason, we might call it the 'new interventionist economics'. It seems to be implicitly assumed that the imperfections that exist in markets do not exist among those who might seek to intervene in markets. Yet it is clear from the crash that regulators suffered from the same herding tendencies as market participants, suffered from lack of perfect knowledge and that there were lags before regulators acted, and so on. Any rounded theory must make realistic assumptions about market participants and those operating outside the market who seek to regulate it. Bounded rationality, radical uncertainty, animal spirits and complexity dynamics are important concepts though; and it is possible to build a more Austrian, less interventionist and more coherent theory on similar foundations to those used by economists proposing greater regulation.

Bubbles

Asset price bubbles are a well-recognised phenomenon in the literature.[1] A bubble exists when an asset's price deviates persistently from its underlying value. The underlying value of a financial asset is the discounted present value of its future cash flows, discounted at an interest rate that reflects risk.

It can be hard to know if there is bubble because an asset's underlying value cannot be objectively assessed. It is relatively easy to determine, however, the underlying value of what investors call a 'closed-end country fund'. Such a fund is simply a fixed basket of shares and bonds specific to a given country. Each component of the country fund has its own price. When you add them up they should just

---

1   Gurkaynack (2008) surveys econometric tests of asset price bubbles.

about equal the price of the fund, after adjusting for things such as differential tax treatment and management fees. However, Ahmed et al. (1997) and Lee et al. (1990) find strong evidence of bubbles in several closed-end country funds in the late 1980s and early 1990s. Thus, there seems to be at least some relatively unambiguous cases of bubbles in modern financial markets.[2] Some experiments with human subjects also suggest that financial markets are generally subject to bubbles (Smith et al. 1988; King et al. 1993; Smith et al. 2000; Lei et al. 2001; Porter and Smith 2003, 2008).

Garber (1990), on the other hand, argues that bubbles are rare to the point of non-existence. Investors in the Dutch Tulipmania (1634–37), the Mississippi Bubble (1719–20) and the South Sea Bubble (1720) were not somehow irrational he suggests. They merely acted on a plausible view of market fundamentals. He offers several explanations for events that look like bubbles, including 'perception of an increased probability of large returns [...] triggered by genuine economic good news, by a convincing new economic theory about payoffs or by a fraud launched by insiders acting strategically to trick investors' (p. 35). According to Garber, 'mania characterizations have served to divert economists from understanding those outlying events highest in informational content' (p. 53). In other words, our 20–20 hindsight should not cause us to falsely impute past price movements to irrational

---

2   Surprisingly, perhaps, bubbles can be consistent with rational expectations. See, for example, Blanchard and Watson (1982).

manias, and a belief in bubbles may be blinding us to other causes of high asset prices in a particular historical situation.

Barlevy (2007: 50) concludes that the theoretical derivation of bubbles requires that 'The potential number of traders who trade in the asset is infinite, traders start out with different prior beliefs or they believe other traders are irrational, or there must be some inefficiency in the economy prior to the initiation of trade.'[3] Frydman and Goldberg (2009: 2011) argue the concept of bubbles – rational or irrational – being wholly separate from fundamental values ignores the underlying process of agents acting with limited information. They contend that 'appealing to manias to explain long swings in asset prices suggests that these movements are an aberration from otherwise 'normal' times,' when, in reality, 'long swings in asset prices are the norm, not the exception' (2009: 35). In their approach, price swings are the result of the relationship between the actions of bullish and bearish investors who act without perfect information and within a corridor of price variation. Policy, according to Frydman and Goldberg, should not aim to eliminate price swings entirely because these swings serve a useful function: namely, discovering the fundamental value. Instead, policy should be designed to dampen excessive price swings (which impose unnecessary costs on society), narrowing the corridor within

---

3 The interested reader should also see Tirole (1982, 1985), Weil (1987), Camerer (1989), Santos and Woodford (1997), Huang and Werner (2004) and Barlevy (2007).

which the discovery process takes place (2009: 20–30, 2011: 217–48).[4]

With regard to asset bubbles, I argue (Koppl 2002) that they are in part a function of the institutional regime. If there is atomistic competition with people acting under stable rules, bubbles will be smaller. Modern asset bubbles, on the other hand, can often be traced to the presence of 'Big Players' in the economic and financial system. Several empirical studies suggest that such a Big Players theory may fit the facts (see Koppl and Mramor 2003; Koppl and Tuluca 2004; Koppl and Sarjanovic 2004; and the earlier studies discussed in Koppl 2002).

Radical uncertainty

Unlike asset price bubbles, radical uncertainty has gained little traction among mainstream economists. Radical uncertainty exists when the future is unknown in the sense that we are unable to assign probabilities to all future possibilities. When we can list the possibilities and assign a known probability to each, the situation is one of 'risk' but not radical uncertainty. For example, if a company has a 50 per cent probability of defaulting entirely and a 50 per cent probability of repaying a loan in full, a bank would face a quantifiable risk. If, on the other hand, it is impossible to assign probabilities to outcomes, there is uncertainty. Investing in the face of uncertainty is more difficult than investing in the face of risk.

---

4   Edmund Phelps (2009: 9) endorses this position.

After the bust Richard Posner (2009) embraced the idea of radical uncertainty. He writes, 'uncertainy – in the sense of a risk that, unlike the risk of losing at roulette, cannot be calculated – is a pervasive feature of the economic environment, particularly with respect to projects intended to satisfy future consumption.' He describes this claim as foundational.

The economics literature already contains the elements required to bring radical uncertainty into the mainstream. While the concept is unlikely to be called 'radical uncertainty', more common labels including 'Knightian uncertainty', 'model uncertainty' and 'ambiguity' convey more or less the same idea.

Ellsberg's (1961) classic study – cited widely in the experimental and neuroeconomics literature – showed that people are averse to ambiguity in a laboratory setting. More recent experimental studies show that people respond differently to risk and uncertainty (Camerer and Weber 1992; Luce 2000). Hsu et al. (2005) use brain studies to investigate the differences between risk and uncertainty. They find that persons respond differently, 'on both the behavioral and neuronal level' to risk and uncertainty (p. 1683). Nevertheless, their results 'suggest a unified treatment of ambiguity and risk as limiting cases of a general system evaluating uncertainty' (p. 1683). In this sense they suggest that there is only a modest difference between risk and uncertainty.

However, there is other work, such as that by Huettel et al. (2006) that tends to suggest that there are differences in how risk and uncertainty are processed at the neuronal level. They suggest that 'ambiguous decision making does not represent a special, more complex case of risky decision making; instead, these represent two types of decision making that are supported by distinct [neuronal] mechanisms' (p. 772). Inukai and Takahashi (2006) concur with that result.

Concerned primarily with the robustness of policy rules, Brock et al. (2007) incorporate model uncertainty into the reporting of policy evaluation exercises.[5] This is a highly technical area of research but one that is readily applicable to policy issues though in the early stages of development. As such, it may play a significant role in the macroeconomics of the coming years.[6]

Animal spirits

The concept of animal spirits has a long history tracing to ancient medicine (Koppl 1991). John Maynard Keynes imported the concept to economics, defining it as 'a spontaneous urge to action rather than inaction' (1936: 161). The term is used widely in economics, though it has no fixed meaning. Keynes's original definition seems to have lost pride of place. Unfortunately, more current meanings tend to be vague and shifting. This ambiguity in the term makes it hard to pin down the connections between animal spirits and investment. The notion of 'animal spirits' is often paired with Hyman Minsky's theory of 'financial fragility'.

---

5 For more on model uncertainty, see Levin and Williams (2003), Brock et al. (2003) and Cogley and Sargent (2004).

6 See Durlauf (2012) for a recent survey.

Howitt and McAfee (1992) define 'animal spirits' as 'random waves of optimism and pessimism that are unrelated to fundamental conditions' (p. 493). This meaning is the one that economists usually have in mind when they discuss animal spirits. It is the meaning I will generally use and which equates animal spirits to the 'state of confidence'. Howitt and McAfee note that interest in the concept of animal spirits so defined 'is often attributed to John Maynard Keynes' but claim that 'it could also be attributed to John Stuart Mill or F. A. Hayek, and that the idea goes back at least as far as Henry Thornton (1802)' (1991: 493–94).

Akerlof and Shiller (2009) provide a salient example of the use of animal spirits in the New Interventionist Economics. They say: 'In modern economics animal spirits' refers to (p. 4):

> a restless and inconsistent element in the economy. It refers to our peculiar relationship with ambiguity or uncertainty. Sometimes we are paralyzed by it. Yet at other times it refreshes and energizes us, overcoming our fears and indecisions.

In this view, animal spirits are all about the psychological and irrational side of economics. They distinguish and examine five aspects of animal spirits, namely: confidence, fairness, corruption and anti-social behaviour, money illusion and stories. It is possible that their innovative use of the term will catch on, but we expect the term will generally be restricted to the first item on their list: confidence, which Akerlof and Shiller describe as a cornerstone of their theory. It is that aspect of animal spirits to which I principally refer in identifying animal spirits as a characteristic of the New Interventionist Economics.

Interestingly, Akerlof and Shiller acknowledge and cite Higgs's analysis of regime uncertainty (pp. 70 and 185). However, they suggest that regime uncertainty has a limited effect on the state of confidence. I think this view is mistaken, and I argue below that regime uncertainty and Big Player influence are important factors shaping the state of confidence. They are right to identify a 'confidence multiplier' whereby improving conditions bolster confidence, which improves conditions further, supporting further improvements of the state of confidence. This self-reinforcing process is more autonomous when confidence is fading than when it is growing. Growing confidence must be ratified by business success, which may not always be possible. In particular, if government-created easy credit buoys animal spirits, then the boom is sure to end in a bust and the disappointment of the expectations upon which it fed.

Akerlof and Shiller are also insensitive to the structural dimension of investment. Not all investment is created equal. Such neglect of the capital structure has been a standard Austrian criticism of Keynesian macroeconomics.

A comment of Hyman Minsky (1992: 5) nicely illustrates the Keynesian neglect of Austrian issues. Minsky says:

> An increasing complexity of the financial structure, in connection with a greater involvement of governments as refinancing agents for financial institutions as well as

ordinary business firms (both of which are marked characteristics of the modern world), may make the system behave differently than in earlier eras. In particular, the much greater participation of national governments in assuring that finance does not degenerate as in the 1929–1933 period means that the down side vulnerability of aggregate profit flows has been much diminished. However, the same interventions may well induce a greater degree of upside (i.e. inflationary) bias to the economy.

Minsky seems to say that government intervention may carry an inflationary risk, but is otherwise a pure gain for the system. He does not seem to recognise the deleterious consequences of Big Players and regime uncertainty on the state of confidence. It seems hard to square this remark from Minsky with the collapse of the Great Recession. We had plenty of 'involvement of governments as refinancing agents for financial institutions as well as ordinary business firms' and yet confidence collapsed anyway. The crisis has been labelled a 'Minsky meltdown' (Yellen 2009). But it seems hard to reconcile Minsky's analysis with the historical record.

Minsky viewed his theory as 'an interpretation of the substance of Keynes's "General Theory"', which, he says, rests upon a speculative-financial paradigm (1975: 55). The core notion in Minsky's post-Keynesian vision of the capitalist economy is that 'stability itself is destabilizing' (1982: 101; 1975: 11). Earlier, we saw Krugman express this idea, saying that in good economic times 'debt looks safe' and 'the memory of the bad things debt can do fades into the mists of history. Over time, the perception that debt is safe leads to more relaxed lending standards' (Krugman 2012:

48). Minsky begins his analysis in an imagined state of calm in which most business borrowing can be repaid out of the firm's cash inflows. These are described as 'hedge financing units' (1992: 7). 'Speculative finance units' can support only their interest payments out of cash inflows. 'Ponzi units' cannot even meet their interest payments without further borrowing. Clearly, as Minsky notes, too much speculative and Ponzi finance creates financial instability. The question is how a modern economy may enter into such a state of financial fragility. Minsky's answer is that 'over a period of good times, capitalist economies tend to move from a financial structure dominated by hedge finance units to a structure in which there is large weight to units engaged in speculative and Ponzi finance' (1992: 8). This inevitable progression is how stability is destabilising.

It is hard to see how Minsky's theory goes beyond the claim that financial crises happen and it is capitalism's fault. It is a theory of the state of confidence that consists principally in the proposition that, in an economy where businesses are free to source their capital from financial markets, if confidence starts out strong it will grow to dangerous heights and then collapse. The theory tells us nothing about the conditions that encourage or discourage 'Ponzi finance' except to say that overconfidence will sooner or later overtake the capitalists. Nor does it say anything about how rapidly the system will move from hedge finance to Ponzi finance. As with some versions of animal spirits we have investor confidence moving up and down for no particular reason in an irregular and unpredictable way. It is hard to see how this 'theory' goes beyond the claim that financial crises do sometimes happen, which is hardly an explanation of why they happen. The human psychology behind the theory seems thin. There is no learning in the system. Contrarians seem to play no significant role. In Minsky's theory, the credit boom has little or nothing to do with the rate of credit injection by the central bank (see Prychitko (2010) for an Austrian critique of this theory).

Complexity dynamics

Mathematical complexity has no one official definition. A good benchmark characterisation, however, is possible. Modern complexity theory uses computers and some relatively recent mathematical techniques to study processes in which many interacting agents generate patterns without any overall plan guiding them. The agents might be people, but they might just as well be plants, genes, molecules or something else. The founding of the Santa Fe Institute furthered an ongoing complexity revolution in the natural and social sciences (Waldrop 1992). The tools of complexity theory have been adopted in economics and seem to be growing in importance within the discipline (Colander et al. 2005). The hegemony of dynamic stochastic general equilibrium models excluded the methods of complexity theory from mainstream macroeconomics. The crisis seems to have encouraged some reconsideration.

Bubbles, radical uncertainty and animal spirits do not imply or require any particular modelling technique. It seems reasonable to expect, however, that economists will rely on the tools of complexity theory to trace out their supposed consequences. In particular we should probably expect models of complexity dynamics to characterise the New Interventionist Economics.

While the term 'complexity dynamics' has no formal and widely agreed precise technical meaning, I use the term to mean any model using complexity theory and tracing out the time path of one or more variables of the system. In spite of a large overlap, complexity and complexity dynamics are not quite the same thing. A model is an example of complexity dynamics only if the dynamics are a central part of what the model is supposed to demonstrate, rather than just the necessary path to the more interesting end state or set of end states. In complexity dynamics, the point is the nature of the ride and not the end point or some other aspect of the system.

At least three considerations support the view that the New Interventionist Economics will feature complexity dynamics. There is a general trend towards complexity theory in economics and all the natural and social sciences. The trend within economics has been chronicled by Colander et al. (2005) and discussed in Koppl (2006). Many have noted that the complexity boom was launched when personal computers started to show up on the desks of college professors. Secondly, complexity models generally have heterogeneous agents. It seems difficult to handle radical uncertainty and animal spirits with representative agent models. Finally, focusing on dynamics seems likely because the aim will be to endogenise bubbles and cycles, showing how they come about.

The informational requirements in a traditional economic model used in a general equilibrium context seem to be unrealistically high (Saari and Simon 1978). This gives us further cause to seek out new models relying on new, computational approaches to modelling social phenomena.

In this context, Kirman thinks 'network topology' is the key to understanding financial fragility. The international financial system has grown more connected, which would ordinarily enhance stability. But a few 'nodes' (i.e. a few institutions) have acquired a disproportionately large number of connections and become 'very central' (p. 18) hubs of the system. Kirman quotes Andrew Haldane of the Bank of England saying: 'This evolution in the topology of the network meant that sharp discontinuities in the financial system were an accident waiting to happen. The present crisis is the materialisation of that accident' (Haldane 2009a: 4, as quoted in Kirman 2009: 18).

Kirman sees this skewed network structure as market failure. Quoting Haldane a second time, Kirman analyses the most recent financial crisis and resulting policy proposals (Haldane 2009a: 31):

> Deregulation swept away banking segregation and, with it, decomposability of the financial network. The upshot was a predictable lack of network robustness. That is one reason why Glass–Steagall is now back on the international policy agenda. It may be the wrong or too narrow an answer. But it asks the right question: can network structure be altered to improve network robustness? Answering that question is a mighty task for the current

generation of policymakers. Using network resilience as a metric for success would help ensure it was a productive one.

I discuss the network models of Haldane and others in greater detail below, and I will criticise the proposals for discretionary financial regulation that those models are used to support.

De Grauwe (2009) provides another example of the sort of complexity dynamics model we expect to characterise the New Interventionist Economics. He introduces an expectational ecology of the sort pioneered by Brian Arthur (Arthur 1994; Arthur et al. 1997) to a stylised version of DSGE-models exemplified by Smets and Wouters (2003). De Grauwe uses three equations and incorporates an agent for whom the probability of switching to a new forecasting algorithm is a positive function of the algorithm's recent relative success. In other words people learn and adapt to recent experience. Causality runs both ways between output and 'animal spirits', which are irregular and unpredictable waves of optimism and pessimism. De Grauwe calibrates the model and compares it favourably to the calibrated rational expectations version. Although the waves of optimism and pessimism are unpredictable, De Grauwe attempts to draw policy implications by searching for parameter values in the Taylor rule that minimise the variances of inflation and output.

There is much to admire in the recent trends in macroeconomics we have been reviewing. The economy is a complex adaptive system, which suggests that we may be wise to use the tools of modern complexity theory (Koppl 2009).

The methods of traditional macroeconomic DSGE models seem ill-suited to the study of complex adaptive systems. In particular, it is doubtful that a representative agent could have 'rational' expectations in a complex economy (Markose 2005; Velupillai 2007): the assumption of radical uncertainty seems more appropriate.

In such an economy bubbles are possible and confidence ('animal spirits') matters. Most of the work along these lines, however, seems to point towards more discretion and activism in economic policy. Such policy conclusions are mistaken. For example, recent network models of financial contagion call for the discretionary regulation of financial markets – literally asking regulators to do the impossible. Unfortunately, the Dodd–Frank Act in the US and similar measures passed or proposed in Europe create the very sort of discretionary regulation of financial markets called for in these network models.

The recent trend towards interventionism

As noted above, representatives of the New Interventionist Economics favour regulatory control of the financial system. Kirman (2009), for example, favourably quotes Haldane on the supposed evils of deregulation. Haldane's speech and other statements (Haldane 2009b,c) include analyses of the causes of the Great Recession. And the sort of economics Haldane is celebrating fits our description of the New Interventionist Economics well. He uses complexity models to represent the Great Recession as a bursting bubble brought on when agents with Knightian uncertainty (p. 4) lost confidence (p. 12) in asset prices. This waning of the animal spirits (p. 24) was a market failure (p. 31) and regulation (p. 4) is needed to improve system performance.

In the US, Janet Yellen, the head of the Federal Reserve System, has described the Great Recession as a 'Minsky meltdown' (Yellen 2009). Yellen explicitly endorses Minsky's model and applies it to the Great Recession. In a remark that might allude to network theory, she says: 'the Minsky meltdown is global in nature, reflecting the ever-increasing interconnectedness of financial markets and institutions around the world' (2009: 6). She goes on to say: 'The severity of these financial and economic problems creates a very strong case for government and central bank action' (p. 7).

Yellen argues in favour of policies to dampen bubbles including through the use of monetary policy (p. 12). She also envisages a greater role for supervision of financial markets, to help prevent excess leverage (an example of what has come to be described as macro-prudential regulation). For example, she argues that capital requirements could be adjusted to provide 'a kind of 'automatic stabilizer' for the financial system' (p. 15). She also recommends differential 'micro-prudential' supervision of 'systemic' institutions: 'Systemic institutions would be defined by key characteristics, such as size, leverage, reliance on short-term funding, importance as sources of credit or liquidity, and interconnectedness in the financial system – not by the kinds of charters they have' (pp. 13–14). Yellen seems to want discretion in the choice of regulatory rules to apply to different financial institutions. Such discretion would push the 'rule of men' (as opposed to the 'rule of law') beyond even the alarming levels Lawrence H. White (2010) chronicles for the Great Recession.

Regulation of the financial markets is a crucial issue. Financial markets are the commanding heights of the modern economy. As we shall see, the Dodd–Frank Act of 2010 creates the sort of discretionary regulation of financial markets advocated by Haldane, Yellen and others. I will try to suggest that this strategy impairs liberty and yet is sure to fail on its own terms. Financial-market regulation is discretionary when the regulatory requirements on a nominally private institution vary from firm to firm in ways that are difficult to rationalise or anticipate, particularly by the affected firms. In the extreme, the nature of the firm's legal charter may not matter and the regulatory requirements on a firm may depend on its identity.

Discretionary regulation is not new in the post-war economies of the democratic West of course. Fritz Machlup criticised US anti-trust legislation for its 'vagueness and uncertainty' which necessarily follow from 'the impossibility of defining such phrases as "unreasonable" restraint of trade' (1952: 183–84). He quotes George Folk noting that 'under the "rule of reason" in the application of the anti-trust laws to any given situation there is no "rule of thumb" to determine the issue' (Folk 1942 as quoted in Machlup 1952: 184). I suppose one might also view discretionary monetary policy as a form of discretionary financial regulation, although that classification would probably stretch the meaning of 'regulation' beyond its proper limits. In any event, the recent financial crisis seems to have made discretion a more important tool in the theory and practice of financial regulation.

Discretionary regulation appears to have become something of a new orthodoxy in the theory and practice of financial-market regulation. I think this orthodoxy is mistaken and dangerous. Discretionary regulation (explained below) violates the rule of law and it tends to make the global financial system more fragile and less resilient.

5   PRE-KEYNESIAN AND POST-KEYNESIAN NOTIONS OF CONFIDENCE

This chapter describes how the idea of confidence was introduced by a number of pre-Keynesian economists and then, despite being given prominence by Keynes under the guise of 'animal spirits', the concept of confidence became more or less lost in the post-war period. Some attention will be paid to the pre-Keynesian literature by way of context and the gist of the theory is present in earlier works such as Higgs (1997), Schultz (1940), Machlup (1939) and Fisher (1933). Although the theory described here contrasts with recent Keynesian theories of animal spirits, this work does draw opportunistically on chapter 12 of Keynes (1936).[1]

J. M. Keynes said of the state of confidence that 'economists have not analysed it carefully' (Keynes 1936: 148). A look at the literature shows that Keynes's complaint was justified. There is no agreed or standard definition of the term and little consistency among economists on its use. We think that the state of confidence is important, but we do not know what it is.

---

1   Keynes, in turn, was drawing at least in part on earlier discussions of 'the state of confidence' as Ritzman (1998) notes.

Ritzman (1998: 171) traces the notion of confidence to Henry Thornton's 1802 work, *Enquiry into the Nature and Effects of the Paper Credit of Great Britain*. While noting the difficulty of deciding just what Thornton meant by 'confidence', Ritzman suggests that it was 'trust in the personal honesty of trading partners and in the stability of the legal system to enforce, if necessary, the fulfillment of contractual obligations' (Ritzman 1998: 171). Ritzman quotes Mill describing the 'unreasonable hopes and unreasonable fears [which] alternately rule with tyrannical sway over the minds of a majority of the mercantile public, [so that] except during short periods of transition, there is almost always either great briskness of business or great stagnation' (Mill 1844: 275, as quoted in Ritzman 1998: 180).

Pigou (1917) links confidence to both money demand and bank reserve ratios. He does not define confidence, but notes that bank reserve ratios and the public's desired money holdings both depend on 'confidence'. When banks have less confidence in the future, they hold more cash relative to the size of their loan portfolio in anticipation of a higher rate of default among their debtors. When the public has less confidence in the future they hold more cash as a 'proportion of their resources' (Pigou 1917: 60).

Miller (1924) links confidence to credit. A crisis of confidence creates a 'break-down of the credit system'. He quotes one author who 'wrote ... of the destruction of confidence by sudden shocks so that "credit no longer serves for cash"' (Miller 1924: 298–99).[2] He summarises the cycle theory of Gouge (1833). According to Gouge, banks expand credit creating a boom, which collapses when many of the notes banks printed are returned for redemption in gold, forcing a contraction of the money supply. Gouge (1833 [1968]: 26) says:

> By the reduction of the amount of Bank medium, the prices of things are lowered, the importation of some kinds of foreign goods is diminished, and specie is brought back. Then the confidence of the Banks is re-newed, and they re-commence their issues of paper. Prices are raised again, and speculation is excited anew. But prices soon undergo another fall, and the temporary and artificial prosperity is followed by real and severe adversity. Such is the circle which a mixed currency is always describing.

In this story, confidence *of* (not *in*) the banks causes a self-reversing expansion of the money supply. I will use a notion of 'bankers' confidence' to tell a similar story. Bellerby (1924) links 'confidence' to price swings. He calls for stabilising the currency with a monetary rule, the 'rigid

---

2   The citation is to 'Dew, Essay on Interest (1834): 17'. Presumably, it refers to Thomas Roderic Dew (1802–46), who published 'Essay on interest, and laws against slavery' in 1834. Dew was a professor at William & Mary College and later its president. Regrettably, true to his time, place and social status, Dew was a 'free-trader and a pro-slavery advocate' (http://scdb.swem.wm.edu/index.php?p=collections/findingaid&id=6541&q=).

normal', which is similar in spirit to the Taylor rule.[3] Kahn (1931: 197) views confidence as potentially 'irrational'. It is telling that he believed: 'There is strong justification for concluding on a priori grounds that the inauguration of an active economic policy would promote confidence rather than upset it'. But he accepts the possibility that 'an extensive policy of public works would promote feelings of distrust. For the state of confidence is a function of what people are thinking, even though their thinking may be completely irrational.' This article is cited by Keynes (1936: 113) and is the source of the multiplier analysis.

Fisher (1933: 342) links confidence to hoarding without explaining what confidence is or to whose confidence he is referring. His debt-deflation cycle begins chronologically with 'mild *gloom*' and a 'shock to *confidence*' (1933: 343). While Fisher lists the shock to confidence as the first event of the cycle, he very explicitly says that the cycle cannot get going unless 'a state of over-indebtedness exists' first (1933: 341, 344). My equilibrium model of the state of confidence discussed below is close to Fisher's debt-deflation model, except that I view overconfidence as a less potent cause of over-indebtedness than Fisher seems to.[4]

---

3 'Whenever the price level rose more than 3 per cent above normal, the bank rate would be raised ... The reverse process would take place if a fall of 3 per cent below normal were reported' (Bellerby 1924: 178).

4 Fisher's debt-deflation theory may be closer than commonly recognised to Hayek's theory of the trade cycle. When Hayek says: 'The utilization of new inventions and the "realization of new combinations" would be made more difficult' without fractional reserves

Haberler (1938: 74) lists the 'lack of confidence due to political risk' as one of the special causes that might 'deter people from investment in spite of profitable opportunities.' This compact statement anticipates my explanation of the long slump, which draws more directly on Koppl (2002) and Higgs (1997). Hicks (1936: 247) equates the state of confidence with 'the desire for liquidity.' Commons (1937) reflects the general confusion about what 'confidence' means when he defines it both as the velocity of cheque account money ('the velocity of debits to individual accounts') and as a subjective state of the 'profit-seeker' found 'in his own mind or derived from what he gets out of the minds of others' (p. 687).

Machlup (1939: 24) defines 'confidence' as 'an aggregate of vague ideas about general prospects of profits or losses'. Unlike Kahn, he seems to think that a public investment programme might dampen confidence because such a programme requires unbalanced budgets and a rising public debt. Machlup's definition underlines just how vague and fluctuating the concept has been in the history of economic thought. Unfortunately, its current incarnation, 'animal spirits', is just as vague and fluctuating.

In the context of agricultural lending, Schultz (1940: 322) equates confidence with 'the elasticity that is shown in the treatment of borrowers during periods when expectations are clouded with uncertainty compared with

---

(1933 [1976]: 191), he comes close to acknowledging Fisher's claim that cycles often begin with 'new investment opportunities' that create 'over-indebtedness' (Fisher 1933: 350).

periods when the outlook is more assuring.' When uncertainty is high, lenders require larger margins. My theory of confidence will emphasise the costs of financial intermediation, which puts it close to the account in Schultz.

Koopmans (1941: 160–61) views the state of confidence as merely one of an indefinite host of 'unmeasurable internal factors' (p. 160). He says: 'The working hypothesis introduced' is that such factors 'are themselves in the end again determined mainly by measurable internal and/or recognizable external phenomena, to a minor extent only by pure chance' (p. 161). In other words, the 'state of confidence' can make no independent appearance in macroeconometric models.

Koopmans's somewhat dismissive treatment of the state of confidence is a precursor of the fate of the concept in post-war macroeconomics. While references to the state of confidence by no means disappear, they become more cursory and, perhaps, less frequent. And the meaning of the term, already vague, becomes even more diffused. Phelps Brown (1949: 49), for example, defines it by a not especially systematic list of things such as the 'trust men had in their leaders [that] affected men's spirits and so their appetite for work' during the recent war. Lauterbach (1950) quotes favourably Keynes's complaint that the 'state of confidence' has not been analysed carefully. There had been much discussion of 'anticipations and uncertainty' in the preceding decade, Lauterbach said, 'but some of this discussion has been in terms of either a rather formal "elasticity of expectations" or a mathematical probability calculation' (p. 34).

Lauterbach's lament reflects the fate of the concept after the war. The term appeared here and there, but it was eclipsed by discussions of expectations, risk and uncertainty. And the discussion of these topics was usually conducted in a rather formal way. This change in vocabulary and methods may have discouraged careful discussion of the state of confidence. Katona and Klein (1952: 12) say:

> Business and consumer confidence are often vaguely mentioned as causing 'deviations' but seldom measured in a scientific manner. Empirical research in business cycles has remained aloof from the treatment of psychological variables mainly because of a supposed inability to measure the appropriate magnitudes.

The concept was tossed about. Because it was not 'measured in a scientific manner,' however, it came to play an ever smaller role in research on business cycles. In spite of the decline in discussion of the concept, Geyer (1976: 402) offers a very suggestive discussion of 'the general state of confidence' in terms of 'doubts about the status quo of the socio-political order, rather than the common uncertainties about the future.'

In the mainstream macroeconomics of the period before the crisis, there is little reference to the state of confidence or any related ideas. As we have seen, some neo-classical models of animal spirits do exist. But such models assume, in essence, that the public's expectations are always right. It seems fair to question whether such models reflect anything that could be properly labelled 'animal spirits' or the 'state of confidence', which would seem to invoke some notion of subjective expectations.

It seems fair to conclude that the term 'state of confidence' has had no clear, stable and scientific meaning in economic theory. Ironically, after Keynes complained that 'economists have not analysed it carefully' (Keynes 1936) disciplined discussion of the state of confidence became even less frequent. Recent treatments of animal spirits are just as vague and shifting as the earlier treatments of the state of confidence. Nevertheless, we can still probably identify four elements that frequently arose in the pre-war discussions of confidence.

6 FROM NOTIONS OF CONFIDENCE
TO A THEORY OF CONFIDENCE

In the early discussions of confidence, the word is often taken to be something related to credit. When confidence is high, banks lend relatively freely and perhaps irresponsibly. When confidence is low, banks restrict lending. Secondly, confidence encourages investment, perhaps by stimulating both the demand for and supply of loanable funds.[1] Confidence also influences the demand for money: when confidence rises, the demand for money falls; when confidence falls, the demand for money rises. Finally, confidence is in some respects a subjective phenomenon: it is somehow about what people are thinking and feeling. When confidence is high, there are subjective feelings of optimism and an exaggerated certainty in a bright future. When confidence is low, there is a feeling of pessimism and an exaggerated uncertainty about the future.

There is more than one way to incorporate these four elements into a coherent theory of confidence. I will identify

---

1 I say 'perhaps' because the old literature was not clear about the mechanisms that translated high confidence into high investment levels and low confidence into low investment levels.

an analytically important element that received somewhat muted treatment in the old discussions of confidence and seems completely absent from current discussions of animal spirits. That element is the costs of financial intermediation. More precisely, I will equate bankers' confidence with the subjective costs of financial intermediation. The notion of bankers' confidence probably does most of the analytical work that we need from the state of confidence. Nevertheless, there are at least two reasons to give the state of confidence a broader meaning. Firstly, past usage of the term does so. Secondly, when bankers' confidence is high, non-bank actors are likely to experience a similar optimism; and, when bankers' confidence is low, non-bank actors are likely to experience a similar pessimism. This correlation is a solid economic reason to retain a relatively broad notion of the state of confidence.

Confidence and financial intermediaries

I will begin the discussion of confidence with a treatment of 'bankers' confidence'. For ease of exposition all financial intermediaries will be described as 'banks'. It is important to recall, however, that commercial banks represent only a fraction of financial intermediaries. Poszar et al. (2012: 7–9) show that in the US the size of the 'shadow banking system' greatly exceeded that of the traditional banking sector in 2007 and may still be about as large today. They prudently emphasise imperfections in their size measure for the shadow banking system, but their study confirms the point that banks are only a fraction of financial intermediaries.[2] Thus, when I speak of 'banks' in what follows, the reader should always imagine the word with scare quotes around it.

There are many costs of financial intermediation, including the costs of finding lenders and borrowers. Bernanke (1983: 257) notes that 'because markets for financial claims are incomplete, intermediation between some classes of borrowers and lenders requires nontrivial market-making and information-gathering services.'[3] An important cost of financial intermediation is the expected value of defaults, which may be reflected in a default-risk premium that the bank requires the borrower to pay. Bankers' confidence is related to the *subjective* costs of financial intermediation, which may or may not correspond to the

---

2   I am unhappy with the term 'shadow banking system', which suggests something irregular, unsavoury and dangerous. The term seems to have been coined by Paul McCulley, who defined it disparagingly as 'the whole alphabet soup of levered up non-bank investment conduits, vehicles, and structures' (McCulley 2007: 2).

3   Reading Bernanke (1983) drew my attention to the independent importance of the costs of financial intermediation for explaining busts and slumps. He says, 'There do not seem to be any exact antecedents of the present paper in the formal economics literature' (Bernanke 1983: 258). He suggests that no previous author 'has emphasized the effects of financial crisis on the real cost of credit intermediation' (Bernanke 1983: 258). Bernanke is probably right to make these comments about the originality of his analysis. But we have seen that Pigou (1917) clearly links confidence to the reserve ratios. Gouge (1833), Miller (1924) and Schultz (1940) all have notions of confidence closely related to bank behaviour. Bernanke (1983) does not distinguish between the subjective and objective costs of financial intermediation.

objective costs of financial intermediation. Banks cannot generally know the relevant objective costs of financial intermediation when they are making their lending and borrowing decisions. Thus, the subjective costs of financial intermediation influence their choices, and the objective costs do not. Past objective costs of financial intermediation may influence the bank's subjective appraisal of the relevant current costs of intermediation. But this role of objective costs is somewhat indirect. Moreover, the import of such past values must be interpreted in light of current circumstances, and there is always more than one reasonable interpretation (Lachmann 1943 [1977]: 67).

Thus bankers' confidence is 'high' if the subjective costs of financial intermediation are 'low' and bankers' confidence is 'low' if the subjective costs of financial intermediation are 'high'. The words 'high' and 'low' are put in quotation marks to remind the reader that something is high or low only with respect to a standard, benchmark, or initial value such as recent realised loan losses.

The consequences of a high or low state of bankers' confidence depend on whether the subjective costs of financial intermediation equal the objective costs of financial intermediation. If bankers' confidence is high, the subjective costs of financial intermediation may be below the objective costs; animal spirits may be waxing; there may be a wave of optimism. It could also be, however, that bankers' confidence is high because the objective and subjective costs of financial intermediation have both fallen. If bankers' confidence is low, the subjective costs of financial intermediation may be above the objective costs; the animal spirits may be waning; there may be a wave of pessimism. Again, it could also be that confidence is low because the objective and subjective costs of financial intermediation have risen together.

There is a tendency towards equality of the objective and subjective costs of financial intermediation, as is argued below. Thus, a high state of bankers' confidence will tend to be self-reversing only if the subjective costs of financial intermediation are driven below their objective level. And a low state of bankers' confidence will tend to be self-reversing only if the subjective costs of financial intermediation are driven above their objective level. If there is indeed a tendency towards equality between the objective and subjective costs of financial intermediation, then external causes that change the objective costs of financial intermediation can produce an indefinite rise or fall in bankers' confidence.

An equilibrium model of bankers' confidence

Assume an initial equality between the subjective and objective costs of financial intermediation – the economy is in some kind of 'normal' state where confidence is neither unusually high nor unusually low. Assume then that, for no particular objective reason, banks become more pessimistic. Their subjective costs of financial intermediation go up, perhaps because they expect a higher loan default rate. By assumption, this pessimism is false and baseless. At first the pessimistic turn is a self-fulfilling prophecy (later I will say why I do not expect this effect to be large). In their new low state of confidence, banks increase their reserve ratios and the volume of available credit shrinks correspondingly; there is a contraction of money and credit. If the contraction is large enough, it may be self-reinforcing and the cause of a Fisherian debt-deflation crisis (Fisher 1933). The contraction of credit creates failures, which raise the subjective costs of financial intermediation further, causing a further contraction of credit and the money supply and more failures, which drive the subjective costs of financial intermediation even higher, and so on.

Even if the effect of the collapse in confidence is large, it will eventually right itself. Output will not fall to zero and once output is no longer falling and businesses failing at an abnormally high rate, the banks will have high reserve ratios but relatively low loan losses and their margins will be large. Competition ensures that these large margins will shrink down to levels consistent with the objective costs of financial intermediation. The objective costs of financial intermediation might now be higher than they were in the initial equilibrium. Old knowledge has become obsolete and the new knowledge, born in a time of uncertainty, is less reliable. Such possibilities are not ruled out by pure economic logic. But there does not seem to be any particular reason for the new equilibrium level of the objective costs of financial intermediation to move significantly from its initial equilibrium level. Indeed, given sufficiently free competition we can expect that the crowdsourcing logic of markets will steer the system to more or less its initial level for the objective costs of financial intermediation. Thus, a baseless increase in the subjective costs of financial intermediation will be self-reversing ultimately.

In considering the effects of a baseless increase in the costs of financial intermediation the possibility that the self-reinforcing process of the initial period might drive the system to low levels of output is not ignored. Such a large shock to confidence is improbable, however. The story here is close to that of Fisher (1933). As we saw earlier, he does not believe a self-reinforcing debt-deflation cycle can get going unless 'a state of over-indebtedness exists' first (1933: 341, 344) and any such initial fragility of the system would require explanation. If bankers (and other financial intermediaries) rely mostly on their own individual judgments, not on general opinion, then a chance decline in the overall state of confidence is unlikely to become a self-referencing collapse of confidence. Bankers are experts in the markets they serve, and experts are subject to overconfidence bias (Angner 2006). Thus, only a special cause seems likely to induce the sort of herd mentality that would make a large collapse in confidence plausible. It seems fair to conclude that any cycles originating in a collapse of confidence will be relatively small in a competitive system. An oligopolistic or heavily regulated system, however, may be less likely to move quickly to its equilibrium level of confidence.

We could also imagine a sudden increase in bankers' confidence and corresponding decrease in the subjective costs of financial intermediation. Such an arbitrary waxing of animal spirits will cause an increase in lending, a reduction in reserve ratios and, therefore, in extreme cases, all the consequences of an Austrian-style boom. But the boom is self-correcting as our earlier discussion revealed. Moreover, a competitive system is unlikely to experience a large jump in confidence without a specific cause. Thus, it seems fair to conclude that any cycles originating in a surge of confidence will be relatively small in a competitive system.

This reasoning therefore somewhat discounts the possibility of an endogenous business cycle in a more or less free market system. But I would not wish to deny the possibility altogether. Hayek (1933 [1976]: 177–92) views cycles as an inevitable consequence of the elasticity of the money supply which, in turn, is a necessary consequence of fractional reserve banking (p. 190): 'They are, in a sense, the price we pay for a speed of development exceeding that which people would voluntarily make possible through their savings' (p. 189). My equilibrium model of bankers' confidence also suggests that cycles can and will happen in market economies with fractional reserve banking.

Catastrophic changes in animal spirits and confidence – market phenomena or caused by external shocks?

The damage wrought by cycles endogenous to the market system seems unlikely to rival that of the Great Recession, let alone the catastrophe of the Great Depression in the US. In other words, the 'animal spirits' explanation for such events is not plausible unless behaviour was distorted by events external to the market. Indeed, Friedman and Schwartz (1963), of course, showed that the Great Depression was brought on by a monetary collapse that we should view as a policy failure, not a market failure.[4] Confidence may have been a key issue in the process, but the change in confidence was not endogenous to the market system.

Selgin et al. (2010) review evidence showing that economic performance was worse under the Federal Reserve System than the prior National Banking system and that performance was little or no better even when we exclude the inter-war period. We have seen that the Great Recession was also a product of unfortunate policy. We will see presently that the slow recovery from each of these events is also attributable to mistaken policies. It would seem, then, that policies intended to improve the economy can backfire by creating a crisis or making it worse. From a comparative institutions perspective, it may be better to tolerate the relatively mild cycles of a largely unhampered market economy than to risk the larger crises that can follow from the attempt to prevent or correct them.[5] We

---

4 Bernanke (1983) identified the costs of financial intermediation as an important real factor aggravating the crisis. Bernanke's important addition to our understanding of the Great Depression does not change the basic contours of the story told by Friedman and Schwartz.

5 I would not speak of 'the' unhampered market, but only of 'largely' or 'relatively' unhampered market systems. To speak of 'the' unhampered market, 'the' free market, or 'the true free market' may easily suggest that only one very specific set of rules is consistent with the economic ideal of free markets or the political ideal of liberalism. But many different sets of rules produce stable property rights, limited government, decentralised decision making and an economic order governed largely by the anonymous forces of supply and demand. The legal rules of any such system will evolve over time as technology and other things change. The notion of 'the'

should prefer robust political economy whereby: 'Relatively large deviations from ideal conditions or the assumptions on which it is based do not result in the collapse of the system but, instead, cause little or no interference with the system's normal performance' (Boettke and Leeson 2010: 102).

When bankers' confidence changes, there are likely to be similar changes in the confidence of the non-bank public, whose responses to events will be similar to those of financial intermediaries. At the same time that bankers' confidence fails, money holders of all types are likely to turn pessimistic as well, causing an increase in the demand for money. When bankers' confidence fails, ultimate demanders and suppliers of credit are likely to be experiencing a similar collapse of confidence, and there will be a decline in both the demand for and the supply of credit.[6] Investors may wish to sell securities, the returns from which depend on business success – such as equities – and retreat to lower risk investments such as government bonds. It may be a matter of taste whether we fold these other decisions into our definition of 'confidence'. As noted above,

---

market might also suggest that slight deviations from the supposedly optimal rule set might crash the system. One of the strengths of liberalism, however, is its robustness, as Adam Smith noted in his criticism of Physiocracy (Smith 1776: 673–74, book IV, chapter 9, paragraph 28). Were the benefits of liberty so fragile, we might be wise to reject it.

6   At the same time, the credit suppliers would demand higher default-risk premia, which would aggravate the decline in the supply of credit.

however, usage seems to suggest the desirability of folding these correlated changes into our notion of 'confidence'.

We can therefore think of the 'state of confidence' as bankers' confidence plus the state of money demand, credit demand and credit supply. This definition brings us closer to 'an aggregate of vague ideas about general prospects of profits or losses' (Machlup 1939: 24) than the more precise idea of bankers' confidence. But it may still be precise enough to support a theory of confidence. Separating out 'bankers' confidence' (the subjective costs of financial intermediation) has the advantage of isolating an element of the system that may not have received as much attention as the demand for and supply of money and credit. Bankers' confidence is not so much a matter of the desired volume of money or investment, but of the system's ability to discriminate between good and bad credit risks. And defining bankers' confidence as the *subjective* costs of financial intermediation helps us to capture the subjective element in confidence, which had been purged from mainstream macroeconomics before the crisis.

7 'BIG PLAYERS' AND THE STATE OF CONFIDENCE

External events can cause changes in the objective costs of financial intermediation. If changes to the subjective costs of financial intermediation follow, then you can have a high or low state of bankers' confidence, and confidence in general, that is not self-reversing. In particular, what will be described as 'Big Players' and regime uncertainty can drive up the subjective and objective costs of financial intermediation indefinitely. As we shall see, the theories of Big Players (Koppl and Yeager 1996; Koppl 2002) and regime uncertainty (Higgs 1997) are not distinct. In both cases uncertainty about policy discourages investment.

The rule of law and atomistic competition create an environment in which people are relatively good at predicting the consequences of their actions. Under the rule of law the rules of the commercial game are relatively simple, stable and understood. When competition is atomistic no one person or small group has disproportionate power in the market.[1] The point about both the theory of Big Players

---

1   The textbook model of perfect competition is one idealisation of atomistic competition in my sense. It is only one among many such

and the theory of regime uncertainty is that bad policy can make it harder, perhaps much harder, for people to predict the consequences of their actions. In that case, both the subjective and objective costs of financial intermediation will be relatively high. This reduces the flow of credit in the system. Thus, bad policy can create a low state of confidence that is not self-correcting.[2]

The impact of Big Players and regime uncertainty

There are two senses in which the rule of law and atomistic competition help people predict the consequences of their actions. Firstly, individuals looking forward have relatively clear and reliable ideas about the consequences of their actions – at least with regard to the kind of outcomes they might expect under different circumstances. Secondly, the filter of profit and loss ensures that the system will respond to events in approximately the way it would have responded if each individual were aware of the events and responded appropriately to them.

When competition is atomistic and the rules of the game are stable, simple and known, then each person can focus attention on underlying scarcities, consumer preferences and so on. Moreover, individuals can narrow their focus to one or a few markets about which they have

---

idealisations, however. Here the term is being used in the more general sense that there are no 'Big Players'.

2 Taylor (2012a: 24, 160) and others have attributed the long slump to uncertainty brought on by bad policy such as the Dodd–Frank Act.

specialised knowledge and good judgement. The stability of the overall environment and the absence of any Big Players allows businesses and individuals to focus on what they know best, thus allowing them to formulate relatively reliable expectations about the future consequences of their present actions.

Even if each person's judgement were highly deficient, the filter of profit and loss causes the system to behave approximately as it would if everyone were smart and informed (see Gode and Sunder 1993; Howitt and Clower 2000). There may be a clustering of errors but not a long-lasting and catastrophic clustering that could explain something like the Great Depression and the boom before it simply in terms of changes in confidence. If wages rise and interest rates fall, for example, profit-seeking firms will substitute capital for labour. What if they don't? Those that stumble into more capital-intensive techniques by chance and those that were already more capital intensive will have lower costs per unit of output. They will accumulate profits and may expand their operations. Firms in the opposite position will have higher costs and may suffer losses. They will be less able to secure credit and may shrink or even fold. The system will shift towards more capital-intensive techniques even if no individual firm self-consciously substituted capital for labour. Atomistic competition under the rule of law lets this filter of profit and loss operate relatively well.

Competition also helps people predict the broad consequences of their actions. However, there are, of course, two ways in which the condition of atomistic competition under the rule of law may be violated: competition may not be atomistic or the rule of law may be absent (later, we will dig a little deeper into the rule of law and discover that these two ways are not distinct).

If competition is not atomistic, there is at least one Big Player in the market. A Big Player has three defining characteristics. The player is big in the sense that its actions influence the market under study; it is insensitive to the discipline of profit and loss; and it is arbitrary in the sense that its actions are based on discretion rather than any set of rules (Koppl 2002: 120). Bigness is necessary to be a Big Player, but it is not sufficient. A Big Player must also be largely free of the discipline of profit and loss. In a reasonably free economy, a big firm may have enough market power to act for a time in arbitrary or inappropriate ways. But if it is not a protected monopoly or, for example, too big to fail, then its deviations from profit-maximising behaviour will eventually cause it to shrink or even fold. But even protected bigness is not enough to make a Big Player. That player must also use discretion rather than simple rules. For example, a single large, protected energy firm that produces energy very inefficiently and sells it expensively to retail distributors of energy may well raise the costs of doing business, but it will not generally contribute to fluctuations in the state of confidence. On the other hand, an activist central bank is a representative Big Player – it can be large, it is protected and its actions will be unpredictable. Large profit-making firms may be Big Players if they are protected monopolies, too big to fail or if they are privileged enterprises in a regulated industry protected from the discipline of profit and loss, but only if they act in an arbitrary way. Government entities are more likely to be big relative to the market and are not generally subject to profit and loss calculation and discipline. Furthermore, in many important instances, they are unconstrained by simple rules. As such, government entities are more likely to be the Big Players that contribute to fluctuations in the state of confidence.

As Koppl and Yeager (1996: 368) point out, discretionary policy tends to reduce the reliability of expectations. This happens because entrepreneurial attention is directed away from more strictly economic factors and, instead, directed towards anticipating changes in and interpreting the wider environment of policy actions that are inherently subject to unpredictable change. Big Players also reduce the efficacy of the filter of profit and loss: chance is more important and sudden arbitrary changes in the business environment are more frequent. The instability produced by Big Players raises the subjective and objective costs of financial intermediation and, in general, lowers the state of confidence. Big Players also encourage herding, contrarianism and increased volatility in financial markets (Koppl 2002: 129–30). Instead of individual firms responding to and interpreting changes in information independently, they focus on the arbitrary decisions of the Big Player and also on how they expect others to react to those changes.[3]

---

3   Editor's note: In financial services in the UK, for example, there have been continual changes to the regime surrounding financial intermediaries (insurance brokers, financial advisers and so on). Instead of such businesses looking downwards towards their

Koppl (2002: 135–38) uses the 'error duration' model of Parke (1999) to model these Big Player effects.[4]

The theory of Big Players has been tested against several different data-sets using a variety of empirical techniques. The evidence seems to support the theory. Koppl and Yeager (1996) study an important episode of Russian nineteenth-century monetary history using data gathered by Yeager, as do Broussard and Koppl (1999) and Koppl and Nardone (2001). These studies show that the ruble exchange rate was more erratic under the interventionist finance minister Ivan Vyshnegradsky than under his more rules-bound predecessor, Nikolai Bunge (see Figure 6).[5] Koppl and Sarjanovich provide evidence that Big Players in agricultural markets cause erratic movements in the international price of wheat.

Such results, and others that can be found in the literature, cannot prove or verify the Big Players theory, of course, but the evidence does seem to support the theory.

---

customers' needs they have been looking upwards towards the regulator and changing their business models in the hope of satisfying the regulator's change of policies.

4   The Parke model also generates the more technical implication that Big Players tend to increase 'persistent dependence' in financial markets.

5   Koppl and Yeager show that 'persistent dependence' increased under Vyshnegradsky. Broussard and Koppl show that unconditional variance increased under Vyshnegradsky, as did the persistence component of the conditional variance in a standard GARCH model. Koppl and Nardone (2001) reach similar results using a unique volatility measure they dub 'X-skewing', which resembles GARCH volatility.

Figure 6   **Ruble exchange rate: German marks per 100 rubles of bank notes**

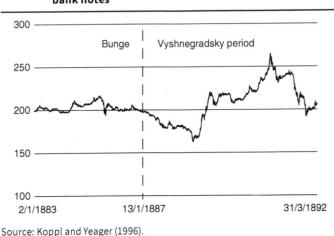

Source: Koppl and Yeager (1996).

More recently, Pástor and Veronesi (2013) have provided further empirical support to the theory by showing that 'Political uncertainty pushes up not only the equity risk premium but also the volatilities and correlations of stock returns' (2013: 4).

Higgs's (1997) theory of regime uncertainty considers violations and prospective violations of the rule of law as a way of dealing with the potentially vague notion of 'confidence'. He says:

> To narrow the concept of business confidence, I adopt the interpretation that businesspeople may be more or less 'uncertain about the regime,' by which I mean, distressed that investors' private property rights in their capital and the income it yields will be attenuated further by government action.

He points out that there are many sorts of actions that might create such distress. They range 'from simple tax-rate increases to the imposition of new kinds of taxes to outright confiscation of private property.' He further notes: 'Many intermediate threats can arise from various sorts of regulation, for instance, of securities markets, labor markets, and product markets' (Higgs 1997: 568). Regime uncertainty is uncertainty about the rules of the game. Regime uncertainty threatens the security of cash flows and increases, therefore, the risk of loan default. Thus, regime uncertainty, like the problem of Big Players, raises the subjective and objective costs of financial intermediation and generally reduces the state of confidence. Higgs (1997) uses his theory to explain the persistence of the Great Depression of the 1930s. Regime uncertainty is not the opposite of 'irrational exuberance' which would be the strong conviction that a bearish position in financial markets will be profitable. Regime uncertainty removes all such firm convictions. It creates doubts about what trades, whether real or financial transactions, bullish or bearish, will be profitable.

Big Players and regime uncertainty both artificially reduce the state of confidence by corrupting the expectations of financial intermediaries and businesses in the real economy. The low state of confidence they create is not self-correcting. As long as the Big Player influence and regime uncertainty persist, the costs of financial intermediation will be high and the flow of credit will be low; the demand for money will be relatively high, and the demand for and supply of credit will be relatively low. In other words, as long as Big Player influence and regime uncertainty

persist, confidence will be low. Big Players and regime uncertainty have the potential to create a permanent slump,
the 'Great Stagnation' as Cowen terms it (Cowen 2011).[6]
When sufficiently entrenched and important, Big Players
and regime uncertainty may create 'crony capitalism'.

Persistent unemployment is not a *necessary* consequence of a long slump created by Big Players and regime
uncertainty. We can imagine a world with high costs of
financial intermediation, but full employment of labour.
Conditions in the modern world, however, make persistent unemployment a *likely* consequence of a long slump.
Unemployment benefits give unemployed workers alternatives to labour.[7] Labour markets are constrained by many

---

6   It is not clear whether Cowen (2011) attributes the great stagnation to bad policy. On the one hand, he says in his opening chapter on 'low-hanging fruit' that the rate of innovation was higher in
the past 'because innovation was easier and it could be done by
amateurs' (Cowen 2011, location 192). This statement and others
seem to say that we've hit a plateau created by objective technolog-
ical possibilities. On the other hand, he says that the mechanism
driving the great stagnation is a shift towards innovations aimed
at 'expanding positions of economic and political privilege, ex-
tracting resources from the government by lobbying, seeking the
sometimes extreme protections of intellectual property laws, and
producing goods that are exclusive or status related' (location 207).
This statement seems to say that we've hit a plateau created by bad
policy. There is also, of course, the separate question of whether
there has been as much stagnation as Cowen claims.

7   Considerations of fairness and compassion may suggest the desirability of unemployment benefits in spite of their tendency to increase unemployment rates, particularly if bad policy is the root
cause of a weak demand for labour. It is worth noting that unemployment in the UK has not been at historically high levels in the

restrictions, including minimum wages and coercive unions.[8]

Keynesian policies tend to create a Keynesian economy

The discussion in this chapter implies that expectations tend to be most prescient when policy is least active and least prescient when policy is most active. In the next chapter, the general ideas laid out so far will be illustrated using the experience of post-crisis policy.

A characteristic feature of Keynes's analysis is the uncertainty of the future: 'The outstanding fact is the extreme precariousness of the basis of knowledge on which our estimates of prospective yield have to be made' (1936: 149). Keynes added that in practice we act as if 'the existing market valuation, however arrived at, is uniquely *correct* [even though] it cannot be uniquely correct, since our existing knowledge does not provide a sufficient basis for

---

Great Recession. However, productivity has slumped. The particular characteristics of the labour market and benefits systems may explain these different responses.

8   If workers can successfully organise without special assistance from the state, there is likely to be good cause to have a union. But if state support is required, unions may lose their voluntary character. This simple principle is hard to apply because employers often enjoy special state benefits. Thus, it can be hard to decide when state support of unions mitigates special corporate privileges created by the state and when, instead, they give unions an inappropriate coercive power. Hayek (1960: 267–84) notes the transformation of labour unions in Britain and elsewhere from oppressed associations to coercive bodies.

a calculated mathematical expectation' (p. 152). Keynes continued (p. 154):

> In abnormal times in particular, when the hypothesis of an indefinite continuance of the existing state of affairs is less plausible than usual even though there are no express grounds to anticipate a definite change, the market will be subject to waves of optimistic and pessimistic sentiment, which are unreasoning and yet in a sense legitimate where no solid basis exists for a reasonable calculation.

Thus, Keynes suggests that in abnormal times in particular, the economy will be driven up and down by baseless sentiments and waves of investor sentiment. Indeed, it is true, as I have argued (Koppl 2002), that we are more disposed to herding the greater our ignorance. But as we have just seen, Big Players and regime uncertainty create and increase the very sort of uncertainty that Keynes described. If we may call such policies 'Keynesian' then we may draw the inference that Keynesian policies tend to create and enhance the irregular ups and downs that Keynes attributed to modern capitalism as such. In this sense, Keynesian policies tend to create a Keynesian economy. Those post-Keynesians who argue for discretionary state intervention as a result of certain features of economic behaviour argue for policies that will increase – rather than reduce – the very behaviours they see as the problem.

The theory of confidence may now make the Great Recession and the long slump easier to understand. The major policy responses to the crisis have created Big Players and regime uncertainty, thus ensuring that the state of confidence is low. In particular, the low state of confidence has discouraged lending and, therefore, the creation of new enterprises.[1] It is not that the animal spirits have waned for no particular reason or for purely psychological reasons, as implied by followers of Keynes. It is more that the subjective and objective costs of financial intermediation have been driven up by the very policy measures undertaken to restore economic health. In this case, as in so many others, policy makers would have served the public better by following some simple advice attributed to Ronald Reagan: 'don't just do something, stand there!'

New work on measuring uncertainty

There has been a growth in academic interest in the concept and measurement of uncertainty in recent years.

---

1   The 'friends, fools and family' that typically support a startup are lenders whose overall lack of confidence may discourage them from supporting an otherwise meritorious enterprise.

Baker et al. (2013: 1) note: 'A rapidly growing literature considers the effects of uncertainty on economic activity'. Baker et al. (2013: 3–4) and Orlik and Veldkamp (2014: 3–5) briefly review this literature, which includes an important strand on 'uncertainty shocks'. This work gives empirical support to the proposition that policy-induced uncertainty is an important cause of the long slump. It tends overall to support the view that the long slump is largely attributable to Big Players and regime uncertainty. See especially the essays collected in Ohanian et al. (2012).

Some crucial findings from this literature include:

- Policy-induced uncertainty makes planning horizons shrink. Investment in the US shifted away from long-term assets and towards short-term assets after the crash. Importantly, this shift is correlated with increases in the US government's budget deficit, suggesting that fiscal activism created uncertainty and discouraged long-term planning and investment (Greenspan 2012). The effect is so strong that 'we have never seen as much aversion to very long-term investments as there is today [in 2012]' (Greenspan 2012, location 394).

- Policy-induced uncertainty reduces growth. The statistical analysis of Baker et al. (2013: 22) shows that the increase in policy uncertainty in the US from 2006 to 2011 probably caused 'a persistent fall in real industrial production' reaching as high as 2.5 per cent at one point.

- Policy-induced uncertainty creates unemployment. The statistical analysis of Baker et al. (2013: 22) also shows that the increase in policy uncertainty in the US from 2006 to 2011 probably caused 'a persistent fall in aggregate employment' reaching as high as 2.3 million jobs at one point. With the US labour force about 155 million persons, that means that policy uncertainty may have added about 1.5 per cent to the US unemployment rate.[2]

The term 'uncertainty shock' seems to have been coined by Greenwald and Stiglitz (1993), who construct a model in which an uncertainty shock will cause a persistent reduction in a firm's output. The recent literature, however, focuses on Bloom (2009) as the origin of recent work on the idea, whose use may be independent of Greenwald and Stiglitz. Building on Bernanke (1983) and Hassler (1999), Bloom finds that firms may respond to an uncertainty shock by 'inaction in hiring and investment'. It is costly to expand *or contract* your labour force or productive capacity. Thus, uncertainty dampens firms' responses to apparent profit opportunities. Firms 'only hire and invest when business conditions are sufficiently good, and only

2   Statisticians are quick to point out that 'correlation is not causation'. In other words, the statistical association between measures of uncertainty and economic variables such as investment, growth and unemployment might exist for a variety of reasons. Baker et al. (2013: 26) note prudently: 'But while the VAR results are empirically robust, it is less clear whether rises in policy uncertainty cause the subsequent drops in economic activity, or simply forecast them because policy making is a forward looking process.' If the overall analysis of this monograph is correct, however, political uncertainty is probably causing declines in planning horizons, employment and economic growth.

fire and disinvest when they are sufficiently bad. When uncertainty is higher, these thresholds move out: units become more cautious in responding to business conditions' (2009: 638). His empirical analysis suggests that the 'zone of inaction' (p. 681) may be large enough to matter. The uncertainty component of one-off events such as 'the Cuban missile crisis, the assassination of JFK, the OPEC I oil-price shock, and the 9/11 terrorist attacks [seemed to create] a 1% drop and rebound in employment and output over the following 6 months' (Bloom 2009: 673).

The work of Bloom (2009) is closely related to that of Baker et al. (2013), who developed a set of indices to measure economic policy uncertainty (EPU). They built their EPU index from components that measure three aspects of economic policy uncertainty. They were (see p. 1):

1. The frequency of references to economic uncertainty and policy in ten leading newspapers.
2. The number of federal tax code provisions set to expire in future years.
3. The extent of disagreement among economic forecasters over future federal, state, and local government purchases and the level of the CPI.

The authors say: 'we find evidence of substantial increases in policy uncertainty in the United States and worldwide since 2007, with our economic policy uncertainty index increasing by more than 50%' (p. 25) (see Figure 7). This increase in policy uncertainty is associated with a slump in output. They find that 'innovations in EPU foreshadow sizable declines in GDP and employment' (p. 25). Recently, Orlik and Veldkamp (2014) have used the

Figure 7   **Index of economic policy uncertainty
(January 1985 to March 2013)**

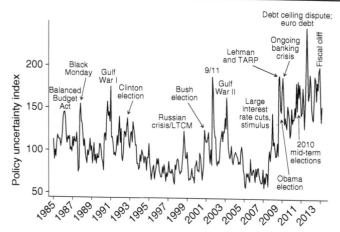

Source: Reproduced by kind permission of Baker et al. (2013), from which this figure is taken.

notion of model uncertainty to help explain the behaviour of the EPU index and broadly similar measures of uncertainty. Swings in uncertainty are not mostly due to exogenous changes in volatility, but to model uncertainty. A sufficiently large surprise causes people to change their models, which will generate relatively large and permanent swings in their beliefs about the future.

Leduc and Liu (2013) correlate the EPU index with changes in the labour market since the Great Recession. They present evidence that heightened uncertainty about economic policy during the recovery made businesses more reluctant to hire workers driving up the rate of unemployment (p. 1). They 'estimate that uncertainty pushed

Box 1 **Policy uncertainty in the UK**

The trends in particular economic variables have been different in the UK from the US and this may be due to differences in tax regimes, labour market structures, and so on. However, the same underlying story is clear – there has been a very long recession and an unusual decline in productivity. From quarter one 2008 to quarter one 2013, annual output growth was –0.7 per cent – an episode that has no modern precedent. There are many reasons suggested for the slump in economic performance. However, it has happened while, according to Baker et al., policy uncertainty has increased in the UK: it increased dramatically after 2008, though has fallen since 2013.[1] During this period there was a dramatic rise in government spending and government borrowing, a process of quantitative easing and very low interest rates. There were also new developments in banking regulation at both domestic and EU level.

During this period of increased policy uncertainty, bank lending to business has been very low in the UK and businesses have been accumulating cash. The former is not surprising given the banking crisis and increase in banking regulation. However, the latter does suggest that businesses are unwilling to make long-term investments. According to one recent report,[2] businesses quoted on the FTSE 100 index increased their cash holdings by over £42bn (34 per cent) in the five years to autumn 2013. This rise in cash holdings has been common throughout the

---

1   See http://research.stlouisfed.org/fred2/series/UKEPUINDX M?rid=279&soid=80

2   http://www.capita.co.uk/news-and-opinion/opinion/2013/ ftse-100-firms-see-cash-piles-climb-since-2008.aspx

developed world and Sanchez and Yurdagul (2013) suggest that it is directly related to uncertainty. Given the obvious relationship between lack of business investment and low labour productivity growth, it would clearly be reasonable to draw a link from policy uncertainty to productivity in the UK context.

the unemployment rate 1.3 percentage points higher by late 2012 than it would have been based on trends from the decade before the downturn. Without elevated uncertainty, unemployment would have been roughly 6.5% at the end of 2012, instead of the actual 7.8%' (Leduc and Liu 2013: 1–2).

What caused policy uncertainty after the crisis?

The list of all the policy responses to the Great Recession is too long to discuss in detail here. There was, for example, the Troubled Asset Relief Program (TARP) and the financial bailout under the Bush administration, including the bailout of AIG. There was the stimulus under Obama and the bailout of the large automobile makers.

An offer they can't refuse

One relatively early response to the crisis is telling in terms of its effect on policy uncertainty. On 13 October 2008 Treasury Secretary Paulson and then-president of the Federal Reserve Bank of New York, Timothy F. Geithner, summoned the chief executives of nine large banks to a meeting.

The situation was described as follows by Lander and Dash (2008): 'To their astonishment, they were each handed a one-page document that said they agreed to sell [preferred] shares to the government, then Treasury Secretary Henry M. Paulson Jr. said they must sign it before they left.' The meeting was less than friendly for at least some of the nine banks: 'It was a take it or take it offer' one participant is quoted as saying. 'Everyone knew there was only one answer.' There was a 'talking points' memo prepared for Secretary Paulson. Some of the language suggests coercion and includes phrases such as: 'Your firms need to agree [to the sales]' and 'We don't believe it is tenable to opt out because doing so would leave you vulnerable and exposed.' This statement was prepared for a group of bank chief executives, at least two of whom (chief executives of Bank of America and Morgan Stanley) insisted in the meeting that they had just raised substantial capital and were not in need of a further infusion (Landler and Dash 2008). They were told: 'If a capital infusion is not appealing, you should be aware that your regulator will require it in any circumstance.'

The apparent coercion of this episode seems hard to reconcile with the image of the detached and neutral regulator. It reveals a government willing to take ad hoc and forceful measures to secure equity positions in strategic enterprises. On the one hand, the government did offer good terms (Landler and Dash 2008). On the other hand it was, as we have seen, a take it or take it offer. The Treasury Secretary and the future Treasury Secretary had made the banks an offer they could not refuse. The symbolic power of this episode may have been quite high for the financial community. In retrospect, it seems an important indicator of the sort of actions the US government was to undertake. And, indeed, the US government did later take equity positions in General Motors and Chrysler, perhaps stoking fears of yet more politicisation of markets.

This response of the government seems to reveal that it was willing to take action based not on any known rules or established procedures, but on the discretion and, perhaps, fear of a few powerful persons. It was an increase in Big Player influence and regime uncertainty. One might have hoped for a return to a more orderly and predictable regime after the heat of the crisis dissipated. Instead, the US Congress passed the Dodd–Frank Act, which further increased Big Player influence and regime uncertainty.

And it is getting worse ... the Dodd–Frank Act

The 849-page Dodd–Frank Wall Street Reform and Consumer Protection Act (2010) contains provisions giving discretionary authority to regulators.[3] The bill creates the 'Financial Stability Oversight Council' or simply 'the Council'.[4] The members of the Council are experts who

---

3   I have often read that the Act is over 2,000 pages in length. This opinion is mistaken and seems to be based on the fact that the last page of the Act as published in the Congressional Record appears on a page numbered 2223. But the first page of the Act appears on page 1375, making the overall length 849 pages.

4   My discussion will be limited to the Council. It will ignore the Bureau of Consumer Financial Protection, which is often associated with Elizabeth Warren. This aspect of the Act seems to create scope for discretion as well.

Box 2 **How TARP encouraged waste, fraud and abuse**

President Bush signed an act creating the Troubled Asset Relief Program (TARP) on 3 October 2008, at the height of the financial panic. TARP authorised $700 billion to be spent on 'troubled assets', which mostly meant mortgage-backed securities that had lost much of their value. The idea was that buying up a lot of 'troubled' securities would somehow create 'financial stability'. It is noteworthy that the law did not provide relief to homeowners, but to their creditors. The seemingly neutral and meritorious goal of 'financial stability' was not to be achieved by helping debtors meet their obligations, but by buying out the creditors directly. Thus, the most innocent victims of the crisis were passed over and creditors such as large financial institutions were given a helping hand.

It seems obvious that TARP would only encourage financial institutions to lend irresponsibly since it holds out the promise of bailout if you get in trouble. And, indeed, the government's own TARP watchdog quickly warned of the dangers of 'moral hazard', which is the tendency to take on too much risk when you know someone else will cover your losses. The report says, tartly: 'Absent meaningful regulatory reform, TARP runs the risk of merely re-animating markets that had collapsed under the weight of reckless behavior' (SIGTARP 2009: 4). TARP seems to have invited fraud as well. Gordon Grigg, for example, helped embezzle almost $11 million from investors 'through false statements, including claims that Grigg was making investments in fictional "TARP-guaranteed debt"' (SIGTARP 2009: 21). Politicians often promise to save taxpayer money by eliminating fraud, waste and abuse. In the case of TARP, however, they *spent* taxpayer money in ways that *encouraged* fraud, waste and abuse. Furthermore, TARP was used to finance, for example, the auto industry bailouts. It therefore turned from being a programme with a specific purpose of stabilisation to a discretionary programme that increased uncertainty while increasing government borrowing.

have been given broad powers in the commanding heights of the modern economy: the financial markets. The Secretary of the Treasury is the chairperson of the Council. The other nine voting members are officials such as the Chairman of the Board of Governors and the Comptroller of the Currency, plus 'an independent member appointed by the President' (Sec. 111 (b), p. 1393).

The Council is empowered to recommend to the Board of Governors of the Federal Reserve System that prudential standards and reporting and disclosure requirements for certain large, interconnected non-bank financial companies and bank holding companies be 'more stringent than those applicable to other non-bank financial companies and bank holding companies that do not present similar risks to the financial stability of the United States' (Dodd–Frank, Sec. 115 (a) (1), p. 1403). When recommending increased stringency the Council may, according to the Act (Sec. 115 (a) (2), p. 1403):

> Differentiate among companies that are subject to heightened standards on an individual basis or by category, taking into consideration their capital structure, riskiness, complexity, financial activities (including

Box 3 **Arbitrary monetary policy**

The unconventional monetary policy of the post crash period has increased uncertainty and Big Player influence.

After the crash, the Fed adopted 'quantitative easing' (QE): buying up long-term securities, mostly long-term Treasury bonds and mortgage-backed securities. The Fed now holds about $1.5 trillion dollars in mortgage-backed securities.[1] Quantitative easing caused bank reserves held with the Fed ('reserve balances') to jump from about $10 billion before the crash to almost $1.5 *trillion* by the middle of 2012 to about $2.5 trillion in early 2014. John Taylor (2012b) has rightly objected: 'The very existence of quantitative easing as a policy tool creates unpredictability, as traders speculate whether and when the Fed will intervene and guess what the impact will be'. Once the Fed's deviation from the Taylor rule resulted in the inevitable crash, it started deviating even further to become a very big player indeed in the market for mortgage-backed securities.

After the crash, the Fed also adopted a policy of 'forward policy guidance', in which it tries to talk markets into lower interest rates by managing expectations. Trying to talk 'sense' into markets just multiplies uncertainty, as we should have learned in the 1990s. On 5 December 1996 Alan Greenspan made his famous remark expressing concern that 'irrational exuberance has unduly escalated asset values' (Greenspan 1996). Given the complexity of asset markets, 'evaluating shifts in balance sheets

---

1   See www.federalreserve.gov/releases/h41/current. It is worth noting that QE in the UK has involved buying government securities and therefore has not intervened directly in private securities markets.

generally, and in asset prices particularly, must be an integral part of the development of monetary policy' (Greenspan 1996). This comment coincided with a notable jump in market volatility. One common measure, the VIX, jumped 70 per cent from under 13 in the year before Greenspan's remark to almost 22 the year after.[2]

2   Author's calculations using CBOE data Accessed from http://www.cboe.com/micro/vix/historical.aspx

the financial activities of their subsidiaries), size, and any other risk-related factors that the Council deems appropriate.[5]

The Act includes a list of the sort of recommendations the Council may make, including risk-based capital requirements, enhanced public disclosures and overall risk management requirements (Dodd–Frank, Sec. 115 (b) (1), p. 1403). The last item especially is vague and open-ended. In making such recommendations, the Council is required to adhere to a list of considerations that includes size, leverage, the 'importance of the company as a source of credit', '[the] nature, scope, size, scale, concentration, interconnectedness, and mix of the activities of the company' and 'any other factors that the Council determines appropriate' (Dodd–Frank Sec. 113 (a) (2) and 113 (b) (2), pp. 1398 and 1399; Sec. 115 (b) (3), p. 1404).

---

5   The Act uses the terms 'systemic' and 'systemic risk' frequently and, I think, rather freely. But it does not use the term 'systemic institutions'.

The Dodd–Frank Act creates a regime of discretionary regulation. Financial market regulation is discretionary when the regulatory requirements on a nominally private institution vary from firm to firm in ways that are difficult to rationalise or anticipate, particularly by the affected firms.

The Act enables regulations that are specific to individual, named firms. Moreover, the considerations for singling out an enterprise include 'any other factors that the Council deems appropriate' and the more stringent regulations may include 'overall risk management requirements'. Thus, we have entered a regime of discretionary financial regulation in which an institution may be targeted for essentially any reason and the measures imposed may be of essentially any nature. This regulation is discretionary in the extreme sense that the nature of the firm's legal charter may not matter (Dodd–Frank, Sec. 102 (a), pp. 1391–92) and the regulatory requirements on a firm may depend on its identity.

Discretionary regulation is not new. It seems fair to say, however, that the Dodd–Frank Act institutionalises a new and higher level of discretion in financial market regulation not least because it gives the regulator the power to interfere in the affairs of a company in respect of its day-to-day operations and not simply with regard to particular (and, perhaps, unusual) behaviours.

It may be clear that Dodd–Frank creates Big Players and regime uncertainty. It may be helpful, however, to demonstrate in some detail that Dodd–Frank violates the legal principle of the 'rule of law'. Doing so will not only help us understand how far wrong US legislators went in the design of Dodd–Frank, it will also allow us to see clearly that Big Players and regime uncertainty are not distinct.

Dodd–Frank and the rule of law

The term 'the rule of law' can be particularly vague and slippery when used in popular discourse. Fallon (1997) has shown, however, that there is a dominant meaning in American legal scholarship.[6] He shows that there is a core meaning common to the varieties of particular meanings that have currency in modern American legal thought.

Fallon gives three values and purposes any conception of the rule of law should serve. A conception of good law that fails on these grounds does not represent a possible version of the ideal of the rule of law (1997: 7–8):

> First, the Rule of Law should protect against anarchy and the Hobbesian war of all against all. Second, the Rule of Law should allow people to plan their affairs with reasonable confidence that they can know in advance the legal consequences of various actions. Third, the Rule of Law should guarantee against at least some types of official arbitrariness.

As far as I can tell, the Hobbesian function of the rule of law is immaterial to the analysis of this monograph. The requirements of predictability and non-arbitrariness do matter, however.

---

6 Fallon's article is an important relatively recent statement of the rule of law. It draws on the classical statement of Dicey (1982). It also draws heavily on Hayek (1944, 1955, 1960).

Based on the three purposes he identified, Fallon lists five elements that, on his reading, the most important accounts generally emphasise (pp. 8–9). Those elements are:

- The rules must be adequate to guide action (i.e. people must be able to understand the law and comply with it).
- The law should actually guide people, at least for the most part, i.e. it should be mostly obeyed.
- The law should be reasonably stable, in order to facilitate planning and coordinated action over time.
- There should be equality before the law (the requirement that justice be blind: 'The law should rule officials, including judges, as well as ordinary citizens').
- There should be fairness, involving due process ('Courts should be available to enforce the law and should employ fair procedures').

Fallon's characterisation of the rule of law is fairly robust: it describes elements that are agreed upon by persons with different legal theories. Dodd–Frank violates the rule of law. It does this not in relation to some abstract detail; it violates the very principle.

The second purpose of the rule of law is violated by the Dodd–Frank Act. The second purpose identified by Fallon was that the people can formulate reasonable expectations about the legal consequences of their actions. The discretionary measures in Dodd–Frank make such expectations difficult to form. The law tasks the Financial Stability Oversight Council with identifying systemic institutions and applying to them potentially idiosyncratic regulations such as more stringent capital requirements. This includes the decidedly vague possibility of imposing 'overall risk management requirements' (Dodd–Frank, Sec. 115 (b) (1), p. 1403).

The considerations that are to guide the Council in determining which institutions to single out for special treatment are also vague. They include 'any other risk-related factors that the Council deems appropriate' (Dodd–Frank, Sec. 113 (a) (2) and 113 (b) (2), pp. 1398, 1399) and 'any other factors that the Council determines appropriate' (Dodd–Frank, Sec. 115 (b) (3), p. 1404). Thus, a financial institution's portfolio and other management decisions are subject to second guessing by a panel of experts that may impose idiosyncratic regulatory requirements that include unexplained 'risk management requirements' and may do so on the basis of any considerations they may deem appropriate. There is no understandable rule here and no predictability. Structural solutions to the problems that law-makers perceive in financial markets, such as requiring that depositors are prior creditors to bondholders when a bank becomes insolvent, may be right or wrong, or good or bad, but they are at least predictable and a business model can be developed around such rules.

Fallon's third purpose of the rule of law is to avoid official arbitrariness. Dodd–Frank, however, introduces arbitrariness in an almost explicit manner. We have seen that it permits the Council to impose more or less whatever measures it chooses on more or less whatever financial institution it chooses. Financial institutions will have to seek the approval of the Council and to curry favour with it.

Fallon's elements of the rule of law are violated as well. In particular, the element of comprehensibility seems to be clearly violated. The opacity of Dodd–Frank is manifest to anyone who has tried to read it. The law calls for 533 rulemakings and 60 studies (Center for Capital Markets Competitiveness n.d.), all of them more or less open ended and unspecified. Financial institutions are uncertain of the law's meaning and struggling to figure it out. The uncertainty associated with Dodd–Frank has been noted repeatedly in the financial press (Bedard 2011; Griffiths 2011; Guerrera 2011; Schoeff 2011; Solomon and McGrane 2011; Unattributed 2011a,b; Wyatt 2011).

Section 619 of the Dodd–Frank Act adds a new section 13 to the Bank Holding Company Act of 1956. This new section is meant to implement the Volcker rule, which would limit proprietary trading and conflicts of interest between financial institutions and their clients. The Dodd–Frank Act required a group of regulatory bodies ('the agencies') to formulate a Volcker rule. The agencies released the proposed rule on 7 November 2011. It includes the following statement: 'In formulating the proposed rule, the Agencies have attempted to reflect the structure of section 13 of the BHC Act ... However, the delineation of what constitutes a prohibited or permitted activity under section 13 of the BHC Act often involves subtle distinctions that are difficult both to describe comprehensively within regulation and to evaluate in practice' (Office of the Comptroller of the Currency et al. 2011: 68849). Thus, the very regulators empowered to execute Dodd–Frank themselves report that the Act is not merely hard to understand, but utterly opaque.

Fallon's second element of the rule of law is that the law should actually guide people. As we have just seen, however, the agencies have declared the bit surrounding the Volcker rule to be difficult to evaluate – so it cannot effectively guide them. And shaping the structure of the financial network, which the Act may bring about, requires knowledge that is not available in principle to financial institutions. Thus, it seems hard to imagine that the Act will be an effective guide to the actions of financial institutions unless they simply take their orders from the regulators. In this case, the law will have transformed private actors into state functionaries. Applying such a principle fully and to all sectors of the economy would create the *Zwangswirtschaft* (Mises 1963: 765) system of socialism, in which the form of private property is retained but not its substance.

Fallon's third element of the rule of law, stability, also seems hard to reconcile with the Dodd–Frank Act. As we have seen, the Act commissions studies and calls for future rules that are not articulated in the Act. Thus, the Act calls for legal changes that are impossible to predict. Even after all studies and all new rules are laid down, the Act still seems hard to reconcile with the principle of stability of the law. As we have seen the Council is tasked with selecting systemic institutions based on 'factors that the Council determines appropriate' and recommending for such institutions special regulatory restrictions for them that may include 'overall risk management requirements'. If market conditions vary unpredictably over time, then the actions of the Council will vary unpredictably as well. Such variability in the recommendations of the Council would compromise the principle of stability.

Fallon's fourth element of the rule of law requires that the law applies to 'officials, including judges, as well as ordinary citizens'. So stated, the Act does not seem to violate this element. We might expand this element to imply a sort of anonymity such that a given legal rule applies equally to an indeterminate number of persons or entities without regard to the circumstances of time and place. Hayek (1960) adopts this view when he contrasts rules and commands: 'Law in its ideal form ... is abstracted from all particular circumstances of time and place and refers only to such conditions as may occur anywhere and at any time' (Hayek 1960: 149–50). While Dodd–Frank clearly violates this aspect of the Hayekian interpretation of the rule of law, we cannot say the same of Fallon's fourth element.

Finally, Fallon suggests that there must be fairness in order for the rule of law to be satisfied. It is hard to apply the concept of fairness to economic regulation in a way that will command assent from a wide variety of observers. The problem is not as bad if we narrow down the idea of fairness, making it more precise and less vague. To have done so, however, would have been contrary to Fallon's purposes. The provisions of Dodd–Frank may or may not be fair, but is not a strong case to be made that Dodd–Frank violates this element of the rule of law.

Fallon (1997: 1) and Hayek (1944) both cite Dicey's *Introduction to the Study of the Law of the Constitution* as the leading exposition of the ideal of the rule of law. Dicey gives three complementary meanings of the rule of law. He says: 'It means, in the first place, the absolute supremacy or predominance of regular law as opposed to the influence of arbitrary power, and excludes the existence of arbitrariness, of prerogative, or even of wide discretionary authority on the part of the government' (1982: 120). Secondly, it means equality before the law. And thirdly, it means in Britain that the (British) constitution does not determine the rights of the people but is, rather, shaped by those rights.

Dodd–Frank violates Dicey's first and primary meaning of the rule of law. The Act gives a central role to the very concept that Dicey found to be excluded by the rule of law: 'wide discretionary authority on the part of the government'. The Act does not violate all 'values and purposes' or all 'elements' of the rule of law as characterised by Fallon (1997). It does, nevertheless, violate some of them and the violations are strong enough to conclude overall that the Act violates the rule of law. Thus, whether we appeal to the authority of the classic theorists of the rule of law or consider a wider meaning current in American jurisprudence, Dodd–Frank can be unambiguously declared inconsistent with the rule of law.

Does the rule of law in financial markets matter?

We should probably pause for a moment to consider the importance of this conclusion. Dodd–Frank literally creates lawlessness in financial markets. It is already a serious matter that any piece of legislation would wipe out the rule of law in a large market sector. But financial markets are the commanding heights of the economy: they are the nerve centre. If monetary calculation is impaired in financial markets, then economic rationality will be compromised throughout the system. The seemingly technical problems of financial market regulation strike at the heart of the market system. It is difficult to predict the precise consequences of the corruptions created by Dodd–Frank, but it seems clear that growth will be reduced.

The essence of the rule of law is the prohibition on discretion. As Dicey said, the rule of law 'means, in the first place, the absolute supremacy or predominance of regular law as opposed to the influence of arbitrary power, and excludes the existence of arbitrariness, of prerogative, or even of wide discretionary authority on the part of the government' (1982: 120). Thus, the existence of Big Players (in this case financial regulators with discretion) and the absence of the rule of law are nearly identical conditions. We have seen that regime uncertainty exists when the rule of law is compromised. We can conclude, therefore, that regime uncertainty and Big Player influence are not distinct.

The Dodd–Frank Act creates Big Players and regime uncertainty. It thus seems sure to produce more harm than good. It may nevertheless be worth elaborating a little on why discretionary regulation cannot achieve its stated ends.[7]

The Financial Stability Oversight Council is a body of experts. Such experts are often imagined to be, somehow,

---

7 It is always possible, of course, that stated ends are not true ends. This point is developed at length in the economic theory of regulatory capture (Stigler 1971; Posner 1974).

above the system and uninfluenced by it. They are detached, disinterested, neutral and unbiased.[8] Moreover, they have the cognitive prowess required to perform their assigned tasks. I have argued elsewhere, however, that we should treat experts as ordinary economic agents (Koppl 2012) who have their own interests and cognitive limitations.

If regulators are human persons like other human persons, they may pursue ends other than the general welfare. For example, they may seek enlarged budgets (Niskanen 1971). Even conscientious regulators may have, for example, risk preferences that differ from those of the public. The potentially dangerous motives of regulators need not be crudely selfish. Good hearted regulators may have more spontaneous sympathy for the Wall Street bankers they deal with regularly than for Main Street citizens they do not know personally.[9] Indeed, there are all sorts of potential motives and cognitive biases within regulatory agencies. They may have a bias towards scandal not emerging (leading them to be too risk averse when regulating while trying to delay the public emergence of problems when they arise); they may have overconfidence in resolving problems by writing rules; they may have a bias against the

---

8   This view is reflected in the network literature of Yellen (2009), Haldane and May (2011), and others.

9   Peart and Levy (2005) and Levy and Peart (2007) have emphasised sympathy, approbation and praiseworthiness as motives of experts. Cowan (2012) has noted the role of identity, as modelled in Akerlof and Kranton (2000, 2002). Such motives might create in regulators a sympathetic bias in favour of the very institutions whose behaviour they are to regulate.

trial and error process of a market economy that allows institutions to fail; and so on.

If regulators are human, they will make mistakes and may have difficulty computing the costs and benefits of different policies. The Dodd–Frank Act gives regulators a difficult cognitive task rivalling that of socialist planning in an economy more generally.

Finally, if regulators are human, their decisions may be biased towards self-serving ends. An obvious bias to fear and expect is one towards greater centralisation and greater state control over the decisions of financial institutions (Higgs 1987: 159–95). Such control serves the bureaucratic interests of the regulators in general. Thus regulators may have an interest in more control, as well as a cognitive bias in that direction that develops regardless of any particular self-interest. Moreover, regulators will be loath to blame themselves when things go wrong. They will sincerely protest that they need more tools, more power and more control in order to prevent future problems.

The Dodd–Frank Act seems to have created regime uncertainty and Big Player effects. It seems fair to conclude that Dodd–Frank is damaging the state of confidence.

9   WHAT IS TO BE DONE?

The economy is in a bad state, as too is economic thought. Our policy response to the Great Recession and the long slump matters. Unfortunately, as I noted at the outset, we are lurching towards greater and greater command and control. If my diagnosis of the problem is right, however, the movement towards command and control is a mistake that threatens the wealth and welfare of the people. We need to restore the rule of law and economic liberalism. We need to take what I will call the 'constitutional turn'.

There has been widespread disillusionment with macroeconomics since the financial crisis. Queen Elizabeth II famously asked at the London School of Economics why nobody saw the crisis coming.[1] A response to the Queen began, at least, to move outside some of the traditional parameters of macroeconomics even though there was the conventional focus on lax regulation.[2] Students

---

1   This was reported widely. See, for example, http://www.telegraph. co.uk/news/uknews/theroyalfamily/3386353/The-Queen-asks-why-no-one-saw-the-credit-crunch-coming.html

2   See http://economistsview.typepad.com/economistsview/2009/07/why-had-nobody-noticed-that-the-credit-crunch-was-on-its-way. html

at Manchester University have been campaigning to be taught economics that deviates from the mainstream new-Keynesian/neo-classical paradigm.[3] This has been incorrectly characterised by many such as the Guardian newspaper as an attack on 'free-market' economics.[4] As those students recognise, and as this monograph discusses, many alternative economic theories critique the extension of financial regulation in recent years and critique both new-Keynesian and neo-classical economics.

While post-war macroeconomics has generally contained strong elements of Keynesianism in various guises, the rigorous attempts to understand the motivation behind and the implications of Keynes's phrase 'animal spirits' have been limited. There was, in fact, a long history of discussion of this concept before Keynes. But any persuasive theory must ask why animal spirits can become so dominant that they hugely distort economies when economic actors would benefit from contrarian action in the face of those animal spirits. Some neo-classical theories attempt to do this, but not convincingly.

It is proposed in this monograph that we need to look more carefully at the way in which Big Players in the economic system can affect confidence as a result of their dominance. They can boost confidence artificially, for example, through loose monetary policy and they can affect

---

3   See their website at http://www.post-crasheconomics.com/

4   It is worth noting the comment from the student group on this article about the group: http://www.iea.org.uk/blog/mathematical -economics-%E2%89%A0-free-market-heterodox-economics -should-%E2%89%A0-marxism

it adversely by creating policy uncertainty. A study of macroeconomics and the behaviour of financial markets, corporations and individuals should therefore include a study of the behaviour of Big Players, the decisions of which affect confidence and can therefore damage growth. We have seen that, since the financial crash, growth has been unusually low. At the same time policy uncertainty has been unusually high. If these two factors are linked, then conventional economics is perhaps missing one of the most important explanations of one of the longest slumps in economic history.

Deregulation by the Big Players?

This perspective does not tell us much directly about specific policies. Giving advice on monetary policy is especially difficult – in a sense, given the structures that we have, all advice is wrong. Certainly, we could repeal the Dodd–Frank Act, rein in government spending and simplify the tax code. But it is not so clear how you unwind the interventionist state. The epistemic dangers of interventionism apply just as well to an attempted process of deregulation (Koppl 2009: 404). Vernon Smith (2008) provides a salient example, namely, deregulation in the wholesale electrical energy market. Deregulation, Smith explains, is 'effected as a planned transition with numerous political compromises'. The political compromises may contain hidden dangers. Smith continues: 'In California [political compromise] took the form of deregulating wholesale markets and prices while continuing to regulate retail prices at fixed hourly rates over the daily and seasonal cycles in consumption'. The disastrous result was the California energy crisis of 2000 and 2001. This failure of so-called deregulation illustrates that change is hard. In his *History of England*, Hume clearly expresses an aversion to violent political changes of all sorts, saying at one point, 'a regard to liberty, though a laudable passion, ought commonly to be subordinate to a reverence for established government' (1983, vol. VI: 533). This 'Humean status quo bias', as we could call it, warns us against incautious or precipitate deregulation of markets. Such caution should be viewed as an implication of Austrian epistemic arguments perfectly parallel to Austrian warnings about the dangers of regulation and control. However, an economist can with greater confidence say a few things about the sort of *economic constitution* we need.

An economic constitution

Keynesian cures have not worked and they invite crony capitalism. The slump will continue if the state of confidence does not improve. Interventionist measures are futile. We need regime stability and there is no substitute for it. To significantly reduce regime uncertainty and Big Player influence we must take the constitutional turn in economic policy. Short-term policy prescriptions or attempts to find a supposed 'correct' rate of money growth or interbank interest rate are as futile as Soviet attempts to find 'correct' prices without market competition.

Fiscal discipline

Firstly, we need fiscal discipline. Uncertainty over how deficits will be financed creates regime uncertainty. It is not clear how a large current and predicted government debt will be financed. Will there be inflation, price controls, default or surtaxes? What will be taxed? Will 'excess' profits be taxed? And so on. The debt crisis will be resolved one way or another and doubt over how it will be resolved creates regime uncertainty. Regime uncertainty tends to depress the state of confidence and to make optimism fragile.

The tendency of government debt to create regime uncertainty shows that the size of the government does matter. Government expenditures must be paid for. If they are large enough, it becomes a problem to pay for them and the government may not be transparent about how much money it is spending or how it will raise the revenues to pay for that spending. Hayek (1979: 51–52) notes:

> a rational decision regarding the services which government is to render [requires that] every citizen voting for a particular expenditure should know that he will have to bear his predetermined share in the cost. Yet the whole practice of public finance has been developed in an endeavour to outwit the taxpayer and to induce him to pay more than he is aware of, and to make him agree to expenditure in the belief that somebody else will be made to pay for it.

If government revenues are not too big, this game of hide-the-tax-bill can continue without much damage to

Figure 8 **US economic policy uncertainty and government activity**

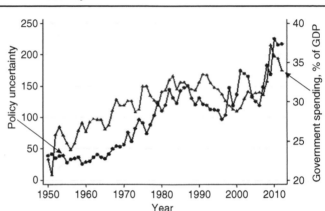

Source: Reproduced by kind permission of Baker et al. (2014), from which this figure is adapted.

the division of labour. But when revenues are big enough, uncertainty over the tax bill becomes destructive regime uncertainty and a drag on output. Baker et al. (2013: 24) say that 'expansion of the Government's role in the economy' is an 'obvious' explanation for the 'clear secular rise in policy uncertainty from the early 1960s until the mid-1980s.' They report a strong correlation between economic policy uncertainty and government expenditures as a share of GDP.[5] Figure 8, adapted from Baker et al. (2014),

---

5 Their explanation is a bit thin. They say only 'correlation 0.812,' without being entirely clear about what two things are being correlated. Presumably, however, they are reporting the R^2 value of a linear regression of the EPU against federal government spending as a share of GDP.

illustrates this. The consequences of deficit spending become self-reinforcing as the state of confidence grows more fragile and self-referential.

An isolated debt crisis can be met with austerity. If it is, the crisis will eventually pass and confidence will return. But if there is a risk that the government will abandon fiscal responsibility, then the state of confidence will be correspondingly fragile and changeable. Given the precariousness of optimism under these assumed conditions, a collapse in confidence is possible and an unconstrained government may find it hard to resist fiscally irresponsible measures.

A monetary constitution

The likelihood of future debt crises would be reduced if current austerity were combined with sensible reforms to create a sound monetary constitution. Just trusting the government to behave is not enough. We should find ways to bind the government more tightly to sound money. Without this the temporary pain of austerity is likely to be too high a price to pay for the long-term benefits it will bring.

What we need is not austerity during crises or, what is more likely, halting and half-hearted austerity during crises. We need monetary stability and confidence that such stability will not suddenly evaporate. This requires a new monetary constitution. Hayek's 1976 essay, on the *Denationalisation of Money*, was explicitly meant to open dialogue on how to create a sound monetary constitution (see p. 20). Hayek noted the likely consequences of creating a new European currency. He said (p. 18):

> It would leave a country with a financially more sophis-
> ticated public not even the chance of escaping from the
> decisions of the others. The advantage of an internation-
> al authority should be mainly to protect a member state
> from the harmful measures of others, not to force it to
> join in their follies.

The recent history of the euro seems to vindicate Hayek's scepticism. Competition is the key to Hayek's thinking about monetary reform. A sound monetary constitution that insulates the economy from Big Player influence requires currency competition.

A regulatory constitution

We also need real regulatory reform. Without a change in the regulatory constitution, as we might call it, there is little hope to escape crony capitalism that increases the role of Big Players. We should regulate the regulators in the same way that markets regulate private firms – through competition. We need what we might call 'rules competition' in regulation, especially the regulation of financial markets. Romano (1998) and Stoll (1998) have outlined plans for competitive regulation of financial institutions. Arthur and Booth (2010) demonstrate how markets used to develop institutions of regulation themselves. Regulatory reform would include restoring competition among ratings agencies. In the run-up to the financial crisis, the position of ratings agencies was privileged through the use of the information they provided in financial regulation and, as such, they became Big Players – they were private sector players, but their privileged position was artificially created by statutory regulators. Just as a sound monetary constitution requires currency competition, a sound regulatory constitution requires rules competition.

The constitutional turn may be considered a Hayekian move. It is also a public choice move. Buchanan and Wagner (1977) applied elementary public choice reasoning to Keynesian policy, concluding that attempts to apply Keynesian policy tilt the system towards chronic deficit spending. Later, Wagner and co-authors (Smith et al. 2011) pointed out that the public and private sectors are entangled. Each sector consists of multiple entities ensnared in various relationships of rivalry and cooperation with other entities, all shaping one another in a dynamic process of mutual adaptation, adjustment and control. The American financial system illustrates the entanglement thesis. Large banks are gambling with other people's money and rationally take on, therefore, more risk than otherwise similar enterprises under a regime that does not invite moral hazard by privatising profits while socialising losses. In this example, the policy regime shapes the risk tolerance of private actors while the risk taking of private actors influences both the individual decisions of regulators and the nature of the overall regulatory regime. 'Constitutional limits on the size of government or on the allowable range of its activities might mitigate some of the disruptive features of entanglement' argue Smith et al. (2011: 65).

To restore the benefits of competition, we must restore competition. There are no substitutes for competition. But competition is hard to maintain because governments have an incentive to encroach on it. The public choice logic of concentrating benefits and dispersing costs culminates in crony capitalism or worse. Democracy has been a check on this logic, but an imperfect check as we have witnessed. The difficulty was recognised long ago by James Madison (1788: 268–69), who gave us what is, in effect, the best short lesson in political economy ever recorded:

> Ambition must be made to counteract ambition. The interest of the man must be connected with the constitutional rights of the place. It may be a reflection on human nature, that such devices should be necessary to control the abuses of government. But what is government itself, but the greatest of all reflections on human nature? If men were angels, no government would be necessary. If angels were to govern men, neither external nor internal controls on government would be necessary. In framing a government which is to be administered by men over men, the great difficulty lies in this: you must first enable the government to control the governed; and in the next place oblige it to control itself. A dependence on the people is, no doubt, the primary control on the government; but experience has taught mankind the necessity of auxiliary precautions.

We have so neglected the necessity of auxiliary precautions in economic policy that policy itself has become ineffective. The current policy ineffectiveness is not that of neo-classical macroeconomics, wherein policy cannot improve upon the best of all possible worlds. It is the policy ineffectiveness of a world in which the state of confidence has become self-referencing and optimism fragile. When confidence is weak and fragile, no rate of money growth is the right rate, no regulatory restriction on banking improves credit markets, and the ordinary policy instruments of the interventionist state stop working. Confidence can be restored, but it may be slow to recover if we are not willing to take the constitutional turn in economic policy.

The constitutional turn does not offer short-term fixes for long-term problems. Elected representatives of the people may not think it is politically possible. It is the duty of economists, however, to speak the truth as they see it. It would be an evasion of this duty if I were to fob off the reader with phoney promises that give the appearance of doing something without effecting real and lasting change. The economy will eventually improve even without the constitutional turn in economic policy. But it will remain subject to business fluctuations that cause needless suffering for ordinary families and threaten to discredit free trade and laissez faire, without which our current wealth and population cannot be sustained.

REFERENCES

AFP (2008) Bush says sacrificed free-market principles to save economy. AFP, 16 December. Accessed 20 September 2011 from http://www.google.com/hostednews/afp/article/ALeq M5jyyKrPjYt7VhpS8G8DrRkr18B0hA

Ahmed, E., Koppl, R., Barkley Rosser Jr, J. and White, M. V. (1997) Complex bubble persistence in closed-end country funds. *Journal of Economic Behavior and Organization* 32(1): 19–37.

Ahrend, R. (2010) Monetary ease: a factor behind financial crises? Some evidence from OECD countries. *Economics: The Open Access, Open Assessment E-Journal* 4, 2010-12, 14 April.

Akerlof, G. A. and Kranton, R. E. (2000) Identity and economics. *Quarterly Journal of Economics* 115(3): 715–53.

Akerlof, G. A. and Kranton, R. E. (2002) Identity and schooling: some lessons for the economics of education. *Journal of Economic Literature* 40(4): 1167–201.

Akerlof, G. A. and Shiller, R. J. (2009) *Animal Spirits: How Human Psychology Drives the Economy, and Why It Matters for Global Capitalism.* Princeton University Press.

Akerlof, G. A. and Yellen, J. L. (1986) *Efficiency Wage Models of the Labour Market.* Cambridge University Press.

Angner, E. (2006) Economists as experts: overconfidence in theory and practice. *Journal of Economic Methodology* 13(1): 1–24.

Arthur, B. (1994) Inductive reasoning and bounded rationality. *American Economic Review* 84(2): 406–11.

Arthur, W. B., Holland, J., LeBaron, B., Palmer, R. and Tayler, P. (1997) Asset pricing under endogenous expectations in an artificial stock market. In *The Economy as an Evolving Complex System II* (ed. W. B. Arthur, S. Durlauf and D. Lane), pp. 15–44. Reading, MA: Addison-Wesley.

Arthur, T. G. and Booth, P. M. (2010) *Does Britain Need a Financial Regulator?* London: Institute of Economic Affairs.

Asso, P. F., Kahn, G. A. and Leeson, R. (2010) The Taylor rule and the practice of central banking. The Federal Reserve Bank of Kansas City Economic Research Department, Research Working Paper 10-05.

Baker, S. R., Bloom, N. and Davis, S. J. (2013) Measuring economic policy uncertainty. Working Paper. Accessed 12 June 2013 from http://www.policyuncertainty.com/media/Baker BloomDavis.pdf

Baker, S. R., Bloom, N., Canes-Wrone, B., Davis, S. J. and Rodden, J. (2014) Why has US policy uncertainty risen since 1960? *American Economic Review* 104(5): 56–60.

Barlevy, G. (2007) Economic theory and asset bubbles. *Journal of Economic Perspectives* 31(3): 44–59.

Bedard, M. (2011) Community bankers speak out on the impact of Dodd–Frank regulations. Loansafe.org, 18 October. Accessed 10 November 2011 from http://www.loansafe.org/ community-bankers-speak-out-on-the-impact-of-dodd-frank-regulations

Bellerby, J. R. (1924) The monetary policy of the future. *Economic Journal* 34(134): 177–87.

Benati, L. (2008) The 'Great Moderation' in the United Kingdom. *Journal of Money, Credit and Banking* 40(1): 121–47.

Bernanke, B. S. (1983) Nonmonetary effects of the financial crisis in the propagation of the Great Depression. *American Economic Review* 73(3): 257–76.

Bernanke, B. S. (2004) The Great Moderation: remarks by Governor Ben S. Bernanke at the meetings of the Eastern Economic Association, Washington, DC. Accessed 2 May 2012 from www.federalreserve.gov/boarddocs/speeches/2004/200402 20/default.htm

Blanchard, O. J. and Watson, M. W. (1982) Bubbles, rational expectations and financial markets. NBER Working Paper W0945.

Bloom, N. (2009) The impact of uncertainty shocks. *Econometrica* 77(3): 623–85.

Boettke, P. J. and Leeson, P. T. (2010) Liberalism, socialism, and robust political economy. *Journal of Markets and Morality* 7(1): 99–111.

Borio, C. and Lowe, P. (2002) Asset prices, financial and monetary stability: exploring the nexus. BIS Working Paper 114.

Brock, W. A., Durlauf, S. N. and West, K. D. (2003) Policy analysis in uncertain economic environments. *Brookings Papers on Economic Activity* 1: 235–322.

Brock, W. A., Durlauf, S. N. and West, K. D. (2007) Model uncertainty and policy evaluation: some theory and empirics. *Journal of Econometrics* 136(2): 629–64.

Broome, L. L. and Markham, J. W. (n.d.) The Gramm–Leach–Bliley Act: an overview. Accessed 17 May 2012 from http://www.symtrex.com/pdfdocs/glb_paper.pdf

Broussard, J. and Koppl, R. (1999) Big Players and the Russian ruble: explaining volatility dynamics. *Managerial Finance* 25(1): 49–63.

Buchanan, J. M. and Wagner, R. E. (1977) *Democracy in Deficit: The Political Legacy of Lord Keynes*. New York: Academic Press.

Calvo, G. (1983) Staggered prices in a utility maximizing framework. *Journal of Monetary Economics* 12(3): 383–98.

Camerer, C. (1989) Bubbles and fads in asset prices. *Journal of Economic Surveys* 3(1): 3–41.

Camerer, C. and Weber, M. (1992) Recent developments in modeling preferences: uncertainty and ambiguity. *Journal of Risk and Uncertainty* 5: 325–70.

Carlino, G. and Defina, R. (1998) The differential regional effects of monetary policy. *Review of Economics and Statistics* 80(4): 572–87.

Center for Capital Markets Competitiveness (n.d.) Dodd–Frank Act of 2010: summary of rulemakings, studies, and Congressional reports by title. Accessed 10 November 2011 from http://www.globalregulatoryenforcementlawblog.com/up loads/file/dodd-frank-summary-sheet[1].pdf

Chari, V. V. and Kehoe, P. J. (2006) Modern macroeconomics in practice: how theory is shaping policy. *Journal of Economic Perspectives* 20(4): 3–28.

Chari, V. V., Kehoe, P. J. and McGattan, E. R. (2008) New Keynesian models: not yet useful for policy analysis. NBER Working Paper 14313.

Christiano, L. J., Eichenbaum, M. and Evans, C. L. (2005) Nominal rigidities and the dynamic effects of a shock to monetary policy. *Journal of Political Economy* 113(1): 1–45.

Clarida, R., Gali, J. and Gertler, M. (1999) The science of monetary policy: a new Keynesian perspective. *Journal of Economic Literature* 37(4): 1661–707.

Clower, R. W. (1965) The Keynesian counter-revolution: a theoretical appraisal. In *The Theory of Interest Rates* (ed. F. H. Hahn and F. P. R. Brechling). London: Macmillan.

Cogley, T. and Sargent, T. J. (2005) The conquest of US inflation: learning and robustness to model uncertainty. *Review of Economic Dynamics* 8(2): 528–63.

Colander, D., Holt, R. P. F. and Rosser Jr, J. B. (2005) *The Changing Face of Economics: Conversations with Cutting Edge Economists.* Ann Arbor, MI: University of Michigan Press.

Cole, H. L. and Ohanian, L. E. (1999) The Great Depression in the United States from a neo-classical perspective. *Federal Reserve Bank of Minneapolis Quarterly Review* 23: 2–24.

Cole, H. L. and Ohanian, L. E. (2000) Reconsidering the effects of monetary and banking shocks on the Great Depression. *NBER Macroeconomics Annual* 15(1): 183–227.

Cole, H. L. and Ohanian, L. E. (2004) New Deal policies and the persistence of the Great Depression: a general equilibrium analysis. *Journal of Political Economy* 112(4): 779–816.

Cole, H. L., Ohanian, L. E. and Leung, R. (2005) Deflation and the international Great Depression: a productivity puzzle. NBER Working Paper 11237.

Commons, J. R. (1937) Capacity to produce, capacity to consume, capacity to pay debts. *American Economic Review* 27(4): 680–97.

Cowan, E. J. (2012) Using organizational economics to engage cultural key masters in creating change in forensic science administration to minimize bias and errors. *Journal of Institutional Economics* 8(1): 93–117.

Cowen, T. (2011) *The Great Stagnation: How America Ate All the Low-Hanging Fruit of Modern History, Got Sick, and Will (Eventually) Feel Better* (Kindle edn). New York: Dutton.

Davis, S. J. and Kahn, J. A. (2008) Interpreting the Great Moderation: changes in the volatility of economic activity at the macro and micro levels. *Journal of Economic Perspectives* 22(4): 155–80.

De Grauwe, P. (2009) Top–down versus bottom–up macroeconomics. Accessed 10 November 2009 from http://www.cesifo-group.de/portal/page/portal/CFP_CONF/CFP_CONF_2009/Conf-es09-Illing/Papers/es09_DeGrauwe.pdf

Dicey, A. V. (1982) *Introduction to the Study of the Law of the Constitution*, Indianapolis, IN: Liberty Classics. (This volume is a reprint of the 8th edn of 1915.)

Durlauf, S. N. (2012) Model uncertainty and empirical policy analysis in economics: a selective review. *Advances in Austrian Economics* 17: 203–26.

Ellsberg, D. (1961) Risk, ambiguity and the Savage axioms. *Quarterly Journal of Economics* 75: 643–79.

Erceg, C. J., Henderson, D. W. and Levin, A. T. (2000) Optimal monetary policy with staggered wage and price contracts. *Journal of Monetary Economics* 46(2): 281–313.

Evans, A. J. (2010) What Austrian business cycle theory does and does not claim as true. *Economic Affairs* 30(3): 70–71.

Fallon Jr, R. H. (1997) 'The Rule of Law' as a concept in Constitutional discourse. *Columbia Law Review* 97(1): 1–56.

Fisher, I. (1933) The debt-deflation theory of Great Depressions. *Econometrica* 1(4): 337–57.

Folk, G. E. (1942) *Patents and Industrial Progress.* New York: Harper & Brothers.

Friedman, M. (1968) The role of monetary policy. *American Economic Review* 58 (March): 1–17.

Friedman, M. and Schwartz, A. J. (1963) *Monetary History of the United States, 1867–1960*. National Bureau of Economic Research Publications. Princeton University Press.

Frydman, R. and Goldberg, M. D. (2009) Financial markets and the state: long swings, risk, and the scope of regulation. *Capitalism and Society* 4(2): 1–44.

Frydman, R. and Goldberg, M. D. (2011) *Beyond Mechanical Markets: Asset Price Swings, Risk, and the Role of the State*. Princeton University Press.

Garber, P. M. (1990) Famous first bubbles. *Journal of Economic Perspectives* 4(2): 35–54.

Garrison, R. (2001) *Time and Money: The Macroeconomics of Capital Structure*. London: Routledge.

Geyer, H. (1976) On the variability of asset preferences. *Finanz-Archiv/Public Finance Analysis* (New Series) 34(3): 389–404.

Giannone, D., Reichlin, L. and Lenza, M. (2008) Explaining the Great Moderation: it is not the shocks. *Journal of the European Economic Association* 6(2/3): 621–33.

Gode, D. K. and Sunder, S. (1993) Allocative efficiency of markets with zero intelligence traders: market as a partial substitute for individual rationality. *Journal of Political Economy* 101: 119–37.

Gouge, W. M. 1833 [1968] *A Short History of Paper Money and Banking*. New York: Augustus M. Kelley. (This edition is a facsimile reprint of the original 1833 edition published in Philadelphia by T. W. Ustick, to which was added an introduction by Joseph Dorfman.)

Greenfield, R. L. and Yeager, L. B. (1982) Money and credit confused: an appraisal of economic doctrine and Federal Reserve procedure. *Southern Economic Journal* 53(2): 364–73.

Greenspan, A. (1996) The challenge of central banking in a democratic society. Federal Reserve Board. Accessed 11 February 2014 from http://www.federalreserve.gov/boarddocs/speeches/1996/19961205.htm

Greenspan, A. (2012) Uncertainty unbundled: the metrics of activism. In *Government Policies and the Delayed Economic Recovery* (ed. L. E. Ohanian, J. B. Taylor and I. J. Wright). Stanford, CA: Hoover Institution Press.

Greenwald, B. C. and Stiglitz, J. E. (1993) Financial market imperfections and business cycles. *Quarterly Journal of Economics* 108(1): 77–114.

Griffiths, T. (2011) Uncertainty over Dodd–Frank rules continues. *Hedge Fund Manager Week*, 20 July. Accessed 10 November 2011 from http://www.hfmweek.com/news/1680342/uncertainty-over-doddfrank-rules-continues.thtml

Guerrera, F. (2011) No jokes: times getting tough for U.S. bankers. *Wall Street Journal* 25 October. Accessed 10 November 2011 from http://online.wsj.com/article/SB10001424052970203911804576650771990385078.html

Gurkaynack, R. S. (2008) Econometric tests of asset price bubbles: taking stock. *Journal of Economic Surveys* 22(1): 166–86.

Haberler, G. von (1938) *Prosperity and Depression: A Theoretcial Analysis of Cyclical Movements* (revised edn). Geneva: League of Nations.

Haldane, A. (2009a) Rethinking the financial network. Speech delivered at the Financial Student Association, Amsterdam. Accessed 10 November 2009 from http://www.finforum.co

.za/fmarkets/200904%20Haldene%20BOE%20Financial%20
networks.pdf

Haldane, A. (2009b) Why banks failed the stress test. Accessed
10 November 2009 from http://www.bankofengland.co
.uk/publications/speeches/2009/speech374.pdf

Haldane, A. (2009c) The systematic risk implications of origi-
nate and distribute. In *Globalization and Systematic Risk* (ed.
D. D. Evanoff, D. S. Hoelscher and G. G. Kaufman), pp. 251–73.
London and Hackensack, NJ: World Scientific Publishing.

Haldane, A. and May, R. M. (2011) Systemic risk in banking eco-
systems. *Nature* 469: 351–55.

Hall, R. E. (2011) The Long Slump. *American Economic Review*
101(2): 431–69.

Hassler, J. A. A. (1999) Variations in risk and fluctuations in demand: a theoretical model. *Journal of Economic Dynamics
and Control* 20: 1115–43.

Hayek, F. A. (1933) [1975] *Monetary Theory and the Trade Cycle*.
Clifton, NJ: Augustus M. Kelley.

Hayek, F. A. (1934) Capital and industrial fluctuations. *Econometrica* 2(2): 152–67.

Hayek, F. A. (1935) [1967] *Prices and Production*, 2nd edn. New
York: Augustus M. Kelley.

Hayek, F. A. (1944) [1976] *The Road to Serfdom*. University of Chicago Press.

Hayek, F. A. (1955) *The Political Ideal of the Rule of Law*. Cairo: Na-
tional Bank of Egypt. (Reprinted in *The Collected Works of F. A.
Hayek*, Vol. 15: *The Market and Other Orders* (ed. B. Caldwell).
University of Chicago Press (2014).)

Hayek, F. A. (1960) *The Constitution of Liberty*. University of Chicago Press.

Hayek, F. A. (1978) The campaign against Keynesian inflation. In *New Studies in Philosophy, Politics, Economics and the History of Ideas*, pp. 191–231. University of Chicago Press.

Hayek, F. A. (1979) *Law, Legislation and Liberty*, Vol. 3: *The Political Order of a Free People*. University of Chicago Press.

Henderson, D. R. and Hummel, J. R. (2008) Greenspan's monetary policy in retrospect. Cato Institute Briefing Paper 109.

Hicks, J. R. (1936) Keynes' theory of employment. *Economic Journal* 46(182): 238–53.

Higgs, R. (1987) *Crisis and Leviathan: Critical Episodes in the Growth of American Government*. Oxford University Press.

Higgs, R. (1997) Regime uncertainty: why the Great Depression lasted so long and why prosperity resumed after the war. *Independent Review* 1(4): 561–90.

Horwitz, S. (2000) *Microfoundations and Macroeconomics: An Austrian Perspective*. New York: Routledge.

Horwitz, S. and Boettke, P. (2009) *The House that Uncle Sam Built: The Untold Story of the Great Recession of 2008*. Irvington, NY: Foundation for Economic Education.

Howitt, P. and Clower, R. (2000) The emergence of economic organization. *Journal of Economic Behavior and Organization* 41: 55–84.

Howitt, P. and McAfee, P. (1992) Animal spirits. *American Economic Review* 82(3): 493–507.

Hsu, M., Bhatt, M., Adolphus, R., Tranel, D. and Camerer, C. F. (2005) Neural systems responding to degrees of uncertainty in human decision-making. *Science* 310: 1680–83.

Huang, K. and Werner, J. (2004) Implementing Arrow–Debreu equilibria by trading infinitely-lived securities. *Economic Theory* 24(3): 603–22.

Huettel, S., Stowe, C. J., Gordon, E. M., Warner, B. T. and Platt, M. L. (2006) Neural signatures of economic preferences for risk and ambiguity. *Neuron* 49: 765–75.

Hume, D. (1983) *The History of England from the Invasion of Julius Caesar to the Revolution in 1688*. Indianapolis, IN: Liberty Fund.

Inukai, K. and Takahashi, T. (2006) Distinct neuropsychological processes may mediate decision-making under uncertainty with known and unknown probability in gain and loss frames. *Medical Hypotheses* 67(2): 283–86.

Jones, D. (2000) Emerging problems with the Basel Capital Accord: regulatory capital arbitrage and related issues. *Journal of Banking and Finance* 24: 35–58.

Jordà, Ò., Schularick, M. and Taylor, A. M. (2011) Financial crises, credit booms, and external imbalances: 140 years of lessons. *IMF Economic Review* 59(2): 340–78.

Kahn, R. F. (1931) The relation of home investment to unemployment. *Economic Journal* 41(162): 173–98.

Katona, G. and Klein, L. R. (1952) Psychological data in business cycle research. *American Journal of Economics and Sociology* 12(1): 11–22.

Keynes, J. M. (1936) *The General Theory of Employment, Interest and Money*. London: Macmillan. (Reprinted in *Collected Writings*, Vol. VII. New York: St. Martin's Press, 1973.)

King, R. G. and Rebelo, S. T. (2000) Resuscitating real business cycles. Rochester Center for Economic Research Working Paper 467.

King, R. R., Smith, V. L., Williams, A. W. and Van Boening, M. (1993) The robustness of bubbles and crashes in experimental stock markets. In *Nonlinear Dynamics and Evolutionary Economics* (ed. R. H. Day and P. Chen). Oxford University Press.

Kirman, A. (1992) What does the representative individual represent? *Journal of Economic Perspectives* 6(2): 117–36.

Kirman, A. (2009) The economic crisis is a crisis for economic theory. Accessed 10 November 2009 from http://www.cesifo -group.de/portal/page/portal/CFP_CONF/CFP_CONF_2009/ Conf-es09-Illing/Papers/es09_Kirman.pdf

Koopmans, T. (1941) The logic of econometric business-cycle research. *Journal of Political Economy* 49(2): 157–81.

Koppl, R. (1991) Animal spirits. *Journal of Economic Perspectives* 5(3): 203–10.

Koppl, R. (2002) *Big Players and the Economic Theory of Expectations*. New York and London: Palgrave Macmillan.

Koppl, R. (2006) Austrian economics at the cutting edge. *Review of Austrian Economics* 19: 231–41.

Koppl, R. (2009) Complexity and Austrian economics. In *Handbook on Complexity Research* (ed. J. B. Rosser Jr). Cheltenham, UK: Edward Elgar.

Koppl, R. (2012) Experts and information choice. *Advances in Austrian Economics* 17: 171–202.

Koppl, R. and Mramor, D. (2003) Big players in Slovenia. *Review of Austrian Economics* 16(2/3): 253–69.

Koppl, R. and Nardone, C. (2001) The angular distribution of asset returns in delay space. *Discrete Dynamics in Nature and Society* 6: 101–20.

Koppl, R. and Sarjanovic, I. (2004) Big players in the 'new economy'. In *Markets, Information and Communication: Austrian Perspectives on the Internet Economy* (ed. J. Birner). New York and London: Routledge.

Koppl, R. and Tuluca, S. (2004) Random walk hypothesis testing and the compass rose. *Finance Letters* 2 (1): 14–17.

Koppl, R. and Yeager, L. B. (1996) Big players and herding in asset markets: the case of the Russian ruble. *Explorations in Economic History* 33(3): 367–83.

Krugman, P. (2010) Martin and the Austrians. *New York Times*, 7 April. Accessed 2 June 2012 from http://krugman.blogs.ny times.com/2010/04/07/martin-and-the-austrians/

Krugman, P. (2012) *End this Depression Now!* (Kindle edn). New York and London: W. W. Norton.

Kydland, F. E. and Prescott, E. C. (1982) Time to build and aggregate fluctuations. *Econometrica* 50(6): 1345–70.

Lachmann, L. M. (1943) [1977] The role of expectations in economics as a social science. In *Capital, Expectations, and the Market Process: Essays on the Theory of the Market Economy*. Kansas City: Sheed Andrews and McMeel.

Lahart, J. (2007) In time of tumult, obscure economist gains currency. *Wall Street Journal* 18 August. Accessed 22 July 2013 from http://online.wsj.com/public/article/SB118736585 456901047.html

Landler, M. and Dash, E. (2008) Drama behind a $250 billion banking deal. *New York Times*, 14 October. Accessed 30 January 2009 from http://www.nytimes.com/2008/10/15/business/economy/15bailout.html

Lauterbach, A. (1950) Psychological assumptions of economic theory. *American Journal of Economics and Sociology* 10(1): 27–38.

Leduc, S. and Liu, Z. (2013) Uncertainty and the slow labor market recovery. *FRBSF Economic Letter* 2013-21, 22 July. Accessed 4 August 2013 from http://www.frbsf.org/economic

-research/publications/economic-letter/2013/july/us-labor
-market-uncertainty-slow-recovery/el2013-21.pdf

Lee, C. M., Shleifer, A. and Thaler, R. H. (1990) Anomalies: closed-
end mutual funds. *Journal of Economic Perspectives* 4(4):
153–64.

Lei, V., Noussair, C. N. and Plott, C. R. (2001) Nonspeculative bubbles in experimental asset markets: lack of common knowledge of rationality vs. actual irrationality. *Econometrica*
69(4): 831–59.

Leijonhufvud, A. (2009) Out of the corridor: Keynes and the crisis. *Cambridge Journal of Economics* 33(4): 741–57.

Levin, A. and Williams, J. C. (2003) Robust monetary policy with
competing reference models. *Journal of Monetary Economics*
50(5): 945–75.

Levy, D. (2009) Public choice for Sheeple. A review of the myth of
the rational voter. *Journal of Economic Behavior and Organization* 69(3): 288–94.

Levy, D. M. and Peart, S. J. (2007) Sympathetic bias. *Statistical
Methods in Medical Research* 17: 265–77.

Levy, D. and Peart, S. (2008) An expert-induced bubble: the
nasty role of ratings agencies in the busted housing market. *Reason Magazine*, 30 September. Accessed 11 November
2009 from http://reason.com/archives/2008/09/30/an-expert
-induced-bubble

Long, J. B. and Plosser, C. I. (1983) Real business cycles. *Journal of
Political Economy* 91(1): 39–69.

Lucas Jr, R. E. (1972) Expectations and the neutrality of money.
Journal of Economic Theory 4(2): 103–24.

Lucas Jr, R. E. (1976) Econometric policy evaluation: a critique. *Carnegie-Rochester Conference Series on Public Policy* 1(1): 19–46.

Lucas Jr, R. E. (1977) Understanding business cycles. *Carnegie-Rochester Conference Series on Public Policy* 5(1): 7–29.

Lucas Jr, R. E. (1980) Methods and problems in business cycle theory. *Journal of Money, Credit, and Banking* 12(4): 696–715.

Luce, R. D. (2000) *Utility of Gains and Losses: Measurement-Theoretical and Experimental Approaches.* London: Lawrence Erlbaum.

Machlup, F. (1939) Period analysis and multiplier theory. *Quarterly Journal of Economics* 54(1): 1–27.

Machlup, F. (1952) *The Political Economy of Monopoly: Business, Labor and Government Policies.* Baltimore, MD: Johns Hopkins Press.

Madison, J. (1788) [2001] Federalist No. 51. In *Hamilton, Alexander, John Jay, and James Madison, The Federalist: A Collection* (The Gideon Edition). Indianapolis, IN: Liberty Fund.

Mankiw, N. G. (1985) Small menu costs and large business cycles: a macroeconomic model. *Quarterly Journal of Economics* 100(2): 529–38.

Mankiw, N. G. (2006) The macroeconomist as scientist and engineer. *Journal of Economic Perspectives* 20(4): 29–46.

Mankiw, N. G. and Reis, R. (2002) Sticky information versus sticky prices: a proposal to replace the new Keynesian Phillips curve. *Quarterly Journal of Economics* 117(4): 1295–328.

Mankiw, N. G. and Reis, R. (2007) Sticky information in general equilibrium. *Journal of the European Economic Association* 5(2–3): 603–13.

Mankiw, N. G. and Romer, D. (eds) (1991) *New Keynesian Economics*, I. Cambridge, MA: MIT Press.

Markose, S. (2005) Computability and evolutionary complexity: markets as complex adaptive systems (CAS). *Economic Journal* 115(504): F159–92.

McCulley, P. (2007) Teton reflections. PIMCO Global Central Bank Focus, August/September. Accessed 29 May 2012 from http://easysite.commonwealth.com/EasySites/EasySite_Z3263Y/_uploads/Teton%20Reflections.pdf

McCulley, P. (2009) The shadow banking system and Hyman Minsky's economic journey. PIMCO Global Central Bank Focus, May. Accessed 22 July 2013 from http://media.pimco.com/Documents/GCB%20Focus%20May%2009.pdf

Meltzer, A. H. (2009) Reflections on the financial crisis. *Cato Journal* 29(1): 25–30.

Mill, J. S. (1844) [1967] On the influence of consumption on production. In *Essays on Some Unsettled Questions of Political Economy*, Vol. IV: *Collected Works of John Stuart Mill*, pp. 262–79. Toronto University Press.

Mill, J. S. (1848) *Principles of Political Economy* (People's Edition). London: Longmans, Green, and Co. Available at http://www.econlib.org/library/Mill/mlP.html

Miller, H. E. (1924) Earlier theories of crises and cycles in the United States. *Quarterly Journal of Economics* 38(2): 294–329.

Minsky, H. (1992) The financial instability hypothesis. Accessed 26 October 2009 from http://www.levyinstitute.org/pubs/wp74.pdf

Minsky, H. (1982) *Can 'It' Happen Again?* Armon, NY: M. E. Sharpe, Inc.

Minsky, H. (1975) *John Maynard Keynes*. New York: Columbia University Press.

Mises, L. von (1963) *Human Action: A Treatise on Economics*, 3rd edn. Chicago, IL: Henry Regnery Company.

Mishkin, F. S. (2011) Monetary strategy: lessons from the crisis. Graduate School of Business, NBER Working Paper 16755, February.

Muth, J. F. (1961) Rational expectations and the theory of price movements. *Econometrica* 29(3): 315–35.

Nelson, C. R. and Plosser, C. I. (1982) Trends and random walks in macroeconomic time series: some evidence and implications. *Journal of Monetary Economics* 10(2): 139–62.

Niskanen, W. (1971) *Bureaucracy and Representative Government.* Chicago, IL: Aldine-Atherton.

O'Driscoll Jr, G. P. (2009) Money and the present crisis. *Cato Journal* 29(1): 167–86.

Office of the Comptroller of the Currency, Treasury; Board of Governors of the Federal Reserve System; Federal Deposit Insurance Corporation; and the Securities and Exchange Commission (2011) Prohibitions and Restrictions on Proprietary Trading and Certain Interests in, and Relationships with, Hedge Funds and Private Equity Funds. *Federal Register* 76(215): 68846–972.

Ohanian, L. E. (2009) What – or who – started the Great Depression? NBER Working Paper 15258.

Ohanian, L. E., Taylor, J. B. and Wright, I. J. (eds) (2012) *Government Policies and the Delayed Economic Recovery.* Stanford, CA: Hoover Institution Press.

Orlik, A. and Veldkamp, L. (2014) Understanding uncertainty shocks and the role of black swans. Accessed 9 February 2014 from http://people.stern.nyu.edu/lveldkam/pdfs/uncertaintyOV.pdf

Parke, W. R. (1999) What is fractional integration? *Review of Economics and Statistics* 81(4): 632–38.

Pástor, L. and Veronesi, P. (2013) Political uncertainty and risk premia. *Journal of Finance* 110(3): 520–45.

Peart, S. J. and Levy, D. M. (2005) *The 'Vanity of the Philosopher': From Equality to Hierarchy in Postclassical Economics.* University of Michigan Press.

Phelps, E. S. (1968) Money–wage dynamics and labor–market equilibrium. *Journal of Political Economy* 76 (July/August, Part 2): 687–711.

Phelps, E. S. (2009) Refounding capitalism. *Capitalism and Society* 4(3): 1–11.

Phelps Brown, E. H. (1949) Morale, military and industrial. *Economic Journal* 59(233): 40–55.

Phillips, A. W. (1958) The relation between unemployment and the rate of change of money wage rates in the United Kingdom, 1861–1957. *Economica* 25 (November): 283–99.

Pigou, A. C. (1917) The value of money. *Quarterly Journal of Economics* 32(1): 38–65.

Porter, D. and Smith, V. L. (2003) Stock market bubbles in the laboratory. *Journal of Behavioral Finance* 4(1): 7–20.

Porter, D. and Smith, V. L. (2008) Price bubbles. In *Handbook of Experimental Economics Results*, vol. 1 (ed. C. R. Plott and V. L. Smith), pp. 247–55. Amsterdam: North-Holland.

Posner, R. A. (1974) Theories of economic regulation. *Bell Journal of Economics and Management Science* 5(2): 335–58.

Posner, R. (2009) How I became a Keynesian. *The New Republic*, 23 September. Accessed 4 November 2009 from http://www.tnr.com/print/article/how-i-became-keynesian

Pozsar, Z., Adrian, T., Ashcraft, A. and Boesky, H. (2012) Shadow banking. Federal Reserve Bank of New York Staff Reports 458, July 2010, Revised February 2012. Accessed, 29 May 2012 from http://www.newyorkfed.org/research/staff_reports/sr 458.pdf

Prychitko, D. (2010) Competing explanations of the Minsky moment: the financial instability hypothesis in light of Austrian theory. *Review of Austrian Economics* 23: 199–221.

Ravier, A. and Lewin, P. (2012) The subprime crisis. *Quarterly Journal of Austrian Economics* 15(1): 45–74.

Ritzman, F. (1998) Money, a substitute for confidence? Vaughan to Keynes and beyond. *American Journal of Economics and Sociology* 58: 167–92.

Rotemberg, J. J. and Woodford, M. (1997) An optimization-based econometric framework for the evaluation of monetary policy. *NBER Macroeconomics Annual* 12: 297–346.

Saari, D. G. and Simon, C. P. (1978) Effective price mechanisms. *Econometrica* 46(5): 1097–125.

Samuelson, A. (1946) Lord Keynes and the general theory. *Econometrica* 14(3): 187–200.

Samuelson, P. A. and Solow, R. M. (1960) Analytical aspects of anti-inflation policy. *American Economic Review* 50 (May, Papers and Proceedings): 177–94.

Sanchez, J. M. and Yurdagul, E. (2013) Why are U.S. firms holding so much cash? An exploration of cross-sectional variation. Federal Reserve Bank of St. Louis Review, July/August, pp. 293–326.

Santos, M. S. and Woodford, M. (1997) Rational asset pricing bubbles. *Econometrica* 65(1): 19–57.

Sargent, T. J. and Wallace, N. (1975) 'Rational' expectations, the optimal monetary instrument, and the optimal money supply rule. *Journal of Political Economy* 83(2): 241–54.

Sargent, T. J. and Wallace, N. (1976) Rational expectations and the theory of economic policy. *Journal of Monetary Economics* 2(2): 169–83.

Schoeff Jr, M. (2011) Politics weighs on economy. *Investment News*, 23 October. Accessed 10 November 2011 from http://www.investmentnews.com/article/20111023/REG/310239980

Schultz, T. W. (1940) Capital rationing, uncertainty, and farm-tenancy reform. *Journal of Political Economy* 48(3): 309–24.

Selgin, G. (2008) Guilty as charged. Mises Daily: Friday, 7 November 2008. Accessed 5 July 2013 from http://mises.org/daily/author/144/George-A-Selgin.

Selgin, G., Lastrapes, W. D. and White, L. H. (2010) Has the Fed been a failure? Cato Institute Working Paper 2, 9 November 2010, revised December 2010. Accessed 29 May 2012 from http://www.cato.org/pubs/researchnotes/WorkingPaper-2.pdf

Shleifer, A. (2009) The age of Milton Friedman. *Journal of Economic Literature* 47(1): 123–35.

SIGTARP, Special Inspector General for the Troubled Asset Relief Program (2009) Quarterly Report to Congress, 21 October, Office of the Special Inspector General for the Troubled Asset Relief Program.

Smets, F. and Wouters, R. (2003) An estimated dynamic stochastic general equilibrium model. *Journal of the European Economic Association* 1: 1123–75.

Smith, A. (1776) [1981] *An Inquiry into the Nature and Causes of the Wealth of Nations* (ed. R. H. Campbell and A. S. Skinner), vol. II of the Glasgow Edition of the Works and Correspondence of Adam Smith. Indianapolis, IN: Liberty Fund.

Smith, A., Wagner, R. E. and Yandle, B. (2011) A theory of entangled political economy, with application to TARP and NRA. *Public Choice* 148(1–2): 45–66.

Smith, V. (2008) *Rationality in Economics*. Cambridge University Press.

Smith, V. L., Suchanek, G. L. and Williams, A. W. (1988) Bubbles, crashes, and endogenous expectations in experimental spot asset markets. *Econometrica* 56(5): 1119–51.

Smith, V. L., Van Boening, M. and Wellford, C. P. (2000) Dividend timing and behavior in laboratory asset markets. *Economic Theory* 16(3): 567–83.

Solomon, D. and McGrane, V. (2011) Regulatory delay stokes unease over Dodd–Frank. *Wall Street Journal*, 7 June. Accessed 10 November 2011 from http://online.wsj.com/article/SB1000 1424052702304563104576363730800713042.html

Stigler, G. J. (1971) The theory of economic regulation. *Bell Journal of Economics and Management Science* 2(1): 3–21.

Stock, J. H. and Watson, M. W. (2003) Has the business cycle changed and why? In *NBER Macroeconomics Annual 2002* (ed. M. Gertler and K. Rogoff). Cambridge, MA: MIT Press.

Suellentrop, C. (2002) Sandy Weill: how Citigroup's CEO rewrote the rules so he could live richly. *Slate*, 20 November. Accessed 17 May 2012 from www.slate.com/articles/news_and_politics/assessment/2002/11/sandy_weill.html

Taylor, J. B. (1993) Discretion versus policy rules in practice. *Carnegie-Rochester Conference Series on Public Policy* 39: 195–214.

Taylor, J. B. (2007) Housing and monetary policy. In *Housing, Housing Finance, and Monetary Policy proceedings of FRB of Kansas City Symposium*, Jackson Hole, WY, September. Accessed 13 May 2012 from http://www.stanford.edu/~john tayl/Onlinepaperscombinedbyyear/2007/Housing_and_Mo netary_Policy.pdf

Taylor, J. B. (2009) *Getting Off Track: How Government Actions and Interventions Caused, Prolonged, and Worsened the Financial Crisis* (Kindle edn). Stanford, CA: Hoover Institution Press.

Taylor, J. B. (2012a) *First Principles: Five Keys to Restoring Prosperity* (Kindle edn). New York: W.W. Norton.

Taylor, J. B. (2012b) Improving the Federal Reserve system: examining legislation to reform the Fed and other alternatives. Testimony before the Subcommittee on Domestic Monetary Policy and Technology of the Committee on Financial Services U.S. House of Representatives, 8 May. Accessed 11 February 2014 from http://financialservices.house.gov/uploaded files/hhrg-112-ba19-wstate-jtaylor-20120508.pdf

Thomas, K. H. (2002) Don't under-estimate the power of Sand Weill. Letter to the editor of *Bloomberg Businessweek*, 30 September. Accessed 17 May 2012 from www.business week.com/magazine/content/02_39/c3801026.htm

Tirole, J. (1982) On the possibility of speculation under rational expectations. *Econometrica* 50(5): 1163–82.

Tirole, J. (1985) Asset bubbles and overlapping generations. *Econometrica* 53(6): 1499–528.

Unattributed (2006) Freddie Mac pays record $3.8 million fine, settles allegations it made illegal contributions between 2000 and 2003. Associated Press, 18 April. Accessed 10 June 2012 from http://www.msnbc.msn.com/id/12373488

Unattributed (2007) Fast and loose. *The Economist*, 20 October, 385(8551): 16–20.

Unattributed (2011a) One year into Dodd–Frank, uncertainty reigns. *Free Enterprise Magazine*, 26 July. Accessed 10 November 2011 from http://www.uschambermagazine.com/article/one-year-into-dodd-frank-still-no-fix-for-financial-ills

Unattributed (2011b) So much for the Volcker rule; even in 298 pages, regulators can't decide what to regulate. *Wall Street Journal*, 25 October. Accessed 10 November 2011 from ProQuest.

UPI (United Press International) (2009) Obama asks Bush to seek $350B rescue funds. upi.com, 12 January. Accessed 20 September 2011 from http://www.upi.com/Top_News/2009/01/12/Bush_will_seek_350B_bailout_if_Obama_asks/UPI-83061231774105/

Velupillai, V. (2007) The impossibility of an effective theory of policy in a complex economy. In *Complexity Hints for Economic Policy* (ed. M. Salzano and D. Colander). Berlin: Springer.

Waldrop, M. M. (1992) *Complexity: The Emerging Science at the Edge of Order and Chaos*. New York: Simon & Schuster.

Weil, P. (1987) Confidence and the real value of money in an overlapping generations economy. *Quarterly Journal of Economics* 102(1): 1–22.

White, L. H. (2008a) How did we get into this financial mess? Cato Institute Briefing Paper 110, 18 November.

White, L. H. (2008b) Did Hayek and Robbins deepen the Great Depression? *Journal of Money, Credit and Banking* 40(4): 751–68.

White, L. H. (2009) Federal Reserve policy and the housing bubble. *Cato Journal* 29: 115–25.

White, L. H. (2010) The rule of law or the rule of central bankers? *Cato Journal* 30: 451–63.

White, W. (2013) The short and long term effects of ultra-easy monetary policy. Accessed 31 July from http://www.oenb .at/de/img/paper_white_tcm14-255924.pdf

Wolf, M. (2010) Does Austrian economics understand financial crises better than other schools of thought? *Financial Times*, 1 April. Accessed 2 June 2012 from http://blogs. ft.com/martin-wolf-exchange/2010/04/01/hello-world/#com ment-1002579

Woodford, M. (2009) Convergence in macroeconomics: elements of the new synthesis. *American Economic Journal: Macroeconomics* 1(1): 267–79.

Wyatt, E. (2011) Dodd–Frank under fire a year later. *New York Times*, 18 July. Accessed 10 November 2011 from http://www. nytimes.com/2011/07/19/business/dodd-frank-under-fire-a-year-later.html

Yeager, L. B. (1997) *The Fluttering Veil: Essays on Monetary Disequilibrium* (edited with an introduction by G. Selgin). Indianapolis, IN: Liberty Press.

Yellen, J. (2009) A Minsky meltdown: lessons for central bankers. Presentation to the 18th Annual Hyman P. Minsky Conference on the State of the U.S. and World Economies. Accessed 11 November 2009 from http://www.frbsf.org/news/ speeches/2009/0416.pdf

Young, A. T. (2009) The time structure of production in the US, 2002–2009. *Review of Austrian Economics* 25(2): 77–92.

ABOUT THE IEA

The Institute is a research and educational charity (No. CC 235 351), limited by guarantee. Its mission is to improve understanding of the fundamental institutions of a free society by analysing and expounding the role of markets in solving economic and social problems.

The IEA achieves its mission by:

- a high-quality publishing programme
- conferences, seminars, lectures and other events
- outreach to school and college students
- brokering media introductions and appearances

The IEA, which was established in 1955 by the late Sir Antony Fisher, is an educational charity, not a political organisation. It is independent of any political party or group and does not carry on activities intended to affect support for any political party or candidate in any election or referendum, or at any other time. It is financed by sales of publications, conference fees and voluntary donations.

In addition to its main series of publications the IEA also publishes a quarterly journal, *Economic Affairs*.

The IEA is aided in its work by a distinguished international Academic Advisory Council and an eminent panel of Honorary Fellows. Together with other academics, they review prospective IEA publications, their comments being passed on anonymously to authors. All IEA papers are therefore subject to the same rigorous independent refereeing process as used by leading academic journals.

IEA publications enjoy widespread classroom use and course adoptions in schools and universities. They are also sold throughout the world and often translated/reprinted.

Since 1974 the IEA has helped to create a worldwide network of 100 similar institutions in over 70 countries. They are all independent but share the IEA's mission.

Views expressed in the IEA's publications are those of the authors, not those of the Institute (which has no corporate view), its Managing Trustees, Academic Advisory Council members or senior staff.

Members of the Institute's Academic Advisory Council, Honorary Fellows, Trustees and Staff are listed on the following page.

The Institute gratefully acknowledges financial support for its publications programme and other work from a generous benefaction by the late Alec and Beryl Warren.

Other papers recently published by the IEA include:

Ludwig von Mises – A Primer
Eamonn Butler
Occasional Paper 143; ISBN 978-0-255-36629-8; £7.50

Does Britain Need a Financial Regulator?
Statutory Regulation, Private Regulation and Financial Markets
Terry Arthur & Philip Booth
Hobart Paper 169; ISBN 978-0-255-36593-2; £12.50

Hayek's The Constitution of Liberty
An Account of Its Argument
Eugene F. Miller
Occasional Paper 144; ISBN 978-0-255-36637-3; £12.50

Fair Trade Without the Froth
A Dispassionate Economic Analysis of 'Fair Trade'
Sushil Mohan
Hobart Paper 170; ISBN 978-0-255-36645-8; £10.00

A New Understanding of Poverty
Poverty Measurement and Policy Implications
Kristian Niemietz
Research Monograph 65; ISBN 978-0-255-36638-0; £12.50

The Challenge of Immigration
A Radical Solution
Gary S. Becker
Occasional Paper 145; ISBN 978-0-255-36613-7; £7.50

Sharper Axes, Lower Taxes
Big Steps to a Smaller State
Edited by Philip Booth
Hobart Paperback 38; ISBN 978-0-255-36648-9; £12.50

Self-employment, Small Firms and Enterprise
Peter Urwin
Research Monograph 66; ISBN 978-0-255-36610-6; £12.50

Crises of Governments
The Ongoing Global Financial Crisis and Recession
Robert Barro
Occasional Paper 146; ISBN 978-0-255-36657-1; £7.50

... and the Pursuit of Happiness
Wellbeing and the Role of Government
Edited by Philip Booth
Readings 64; ISBN 978-0-255-36656-4; £12.50

Public Choice – A Primer
Eamonn Butler
Occasional Paper 147; ISBN 978-0-255-36650-2; £10.00

The Profit Motive in Education: Continuing the Revolution
Edited by James B. Stanfield
Readings 65; ISBN 978-0-255-36646-5; £12.50

Which Road Ahead – Government or Market?
Oliver Knipping & Richard Wellings
Hobart Paper 171; ISBN 978-0-255-36619-9; £10.00

The Future of the Commons
Beyond Market Failure and Government Regulation
Elinor Ostrom et al.
Occasional Paper 148; ISBN 978-0-255-36653-3; £10.00

Redefining the Poverty Debate
Why a War on Markets Is No Substitute for a War on Poverty
Kristian Niemietz
Research Monograph 67; ISBN 978-0-255-36652-6; £12.50

The Euro – the Beginning, the Middle … and the End?
Edited by Philip Booth
Hobart Paperback 39; ISBN 978-0-255-36680-9; £12.50

The Shadow Economy
Friedrich Schneider & Colin C. Williams
Hobart Paper 172; ISBN 978-0-255-36674-8; £12.50

Quack Policy
Abusing Science in the Cause of Paternalism
Jamie Whyte
Hobart Paper 173; ISBN 978-0-255-36673-1; £10.00

Foundations of a Free Society
Eamonn Butler
Occasional Paper 149; ISBN 978-0-255-36687-8; £12.50

The Government Debt Iceberg
Jagadeesh Gokhale
Research Monograph 68; ISBN 978-0-255-36666-3; £10.00

A U-Turn on the Road to Serfdom
Grover Norquist
Occasional Paper 150; ISBN 978-0-255-36686-1; £10.00

New Private Monies – A Bit-Part Player?
Kevin Dowd
Hobart Paper 174; ISBN 978-0-255-36694-6; £10.00

Other IEA publications

Comprehensive information on other publications and the wider work of the IEA can be found at www.iea.org.uk. To order any publication please see below.

Personal customers

Orders from personal customers should be directed to the IEA:

Clare Rusbridge
IEA
2 Lord North Street
FREEPOST LON10168
London SW1P 3YZ
Tel: 020 7799 8907. Fax: 020 7799 2137
Email: sales@iea.org.uk

Trade customers

All orders from the book trade should be directed to the IEA's distributor:

NBN International (IEA Orders)
Orders Dept.
NBN International
10 Thornbury Road
Plymouth PL6 7PP
Tel: 01752 202301, Fax: 01752 202333
Email: orders@nbninternational.com

IEA subscriptions

The IEA also offers a subscription service to its publications. For a single annual payment (currently £42.00 in the UK), subscribers receive every monograph the IEA publishes. For more information please contact:

Clare Rusbridge
Subscriptions
IEA
2 Lord North Street
FREEPOST LON10168
London SW1P 3YZ
Tel: 020 7799 8907, Fax: 020 7799 2137
Email: crusbridge@iea.org.uk